Kitchen Sanctuary

QUICK & EASY

DELICIOUS 30-MINUTE DINNERS

An Hachette UK company
www.hachette.co.uk

First published in Great Britain in 2024
by Kyle Books, an imprint of
Octopus Publishing Group Limited
Carmelite House
50 Victoria Embankment
London EC4Y 0DZ
www.octopusbooks.co.uk

ISBN: 9781804191002

Distributed in the US by
Hachette Book Group,
1290 Avenue of the Americas,
4th and 5th Floors,
New York, NY 10104

Distributed in Canada by
Canadian Manda Group,
664 Annette St., Toronto,
Ontario, Canada M6S 2C8

Publishing Director: Judith Hannam
Publisher: Joanna Copestick
Project Editor: Samhita Foria
Design: Paul Palmer-Edwards
Production: Emily Noto

Printed and bound in China

10 9 8 7 6 5 4 3 2 1

Dedication

This book is dedicated to my mum, who sadly passed away in 2022 from motor neurone disease.

Mum was always super-proud of Kitchen Sanctuary and she took great joy in taste-testing lots of the recipes from my previous book (*It's All About Dinner*).

She passed away just before I started writing this book, but she happily listened to me telling her all about my plans and recipe ideas, and I know she would have loved to help with the taste-testing of this one – especially the Fantastic Fish section!

Love you Mum x

Contents

Introduction

While I absolutely love spending time cooking recipes in the kitchen, it's simply not practical to spend hours in there every day. In fact, most days it's a rush to get dinner on the table in the quickest time possible. However, I don't want to sacrifice flavour in order to get a meal finished faster, so I'm always looking for shortcuts to speed up and simplify the process, without compromising on taste. After all, 'Quick and Easy' is the title of this book. So, if you're reading this and you're finding family life, work, school, etc leaves you with barely any time, you're no doubt looking for ideas to speed up the cooking process too, and that's why I've written this book. So let's get cooking!

In addition to some of the most popular quick recipes on my website, this book has 70 brand-new dishes to see you through every quick-dinner-required scenario!

Why should this book be on your bookshelf?

I would love this to be your go-to book for when you're short on time for getting dinner ready. All the recipes should take you 30 minutes or less to prepare and cook. I've got a whole section on shortcuts that you can incorporate into your everyday cooking, as well as incorporating lots of little shortcuts along the way in my recipes. As far as I'm concerned, shortcuts and quick-to-cook ingredients are great, but in addition to the time-saving element, they MUST deliver on flavour. That's been my motto throughout the whole writing and testing process for this book. It's all about fast flavour!

Notes

- All oven temperatures in degrees Centigrade are the fan setting. If your oven does not have this feature, increase the temperature by 20°C.
- Unless otherwise stated, salt is regular table salt and pepper is freshly ground black pepper.
- If soy sauce isn't listed as 'light' or 'dark' soy sauce, it means 'standard' soy sauce. Use light soy sauce as a replacement if you don't have standard soy sauce.
- If a specific oil isn't stated, use any neutral oil, such as avocado, rapeseed, vegetable or sunflower.
- If you make homemade stock, that's great, but water plus stock (bouillon) cubes will work just fine too.
- I use full-fat dairy (milk, cream, butter, yogurt, cheese) and full-fat coconut milk and coconut cream as I find they taste better and full-fat versions are a lot less likely to split when heated.
- The 30-minute timing is intended to be an average prep and cook time. Naturally some people take longer to prepare ingredients, some ovens and hobs cook at slightly different temperatures (which can add to the overall cook time) and differences in some ingredients (such as meat/fish that come in different sizes) can also affect cooking time.

> ▣ *Check out the videos!*
>
> Not only does each recipe in this book have a photo, but I've included a QR code for EVERY SINGLE RECIPE, that will take you through to a video, so you can see how the recipe is made, every step of the way.

About Nicky and Kitchen Sanctuary

Nicky grew up in Southport, in northwest England, before moving to Staffordshire, where she got her degree in Computing Science. After university, she spent 14 years in corporate IT, where she met husband Chris. They have two children, Gracey and Lewis.

Food and cooking have been a passion for Nicky since age 11, when she first started cooking for her family. She started Kitchen Sanctuary in 2014, initially to diarize her recipes and as a way to relax after a long day in the office. The recipes proved popular with readers and the site started to grow, eventually allowing Nicky to work on it full-time.

In 2017 Chris quit his corporate job to join Nicky working on Kitchen Sanctuary and that's when they started making recipe videos for their YouTube channel.

Kitchen Sanctuary is now one of the most popular recipe websites in the UK, with a readership in the millions every month. The Kitchen Sanctuary YouTube channel is also growing rapidly, with recipe videos being added every week.

Smart Shortcuts

There's no shame in using shortcuts to help speed up a recipe – it's all about personal preference. For some, this might mean using ready-minced ginger or microwave rice, for others it might involve buying a fajita kit with a rotisserie chicken, a bag of salad and some ready-grated (pre-shredded) cheese. It's whatever works for you!

Ready-made/ready-prepped ingredient shortcuts

Some of the things you might want to consider when using ready-prepped ingredients include:

- How much help you need to speed things up – Do you want ready-chopped or ready-cooked ingredients? Do you want one speed-up ingredient, or multiple?
- Whether you're happy with extra additives (flavour enhancers, preservatives etc) that might come with some ingredients – especially sauces, heavily flavoured items or almost full complete ingredients/items (for example soups, filled ravioli, meats cooked in sauces). I try and keep these to a minimum, if I can, but that's not always possible on the busiest days.
- If the taste is better or worse when using a ready-prepped ingredient.

Some examples of items I use on those extra-busy days are:

- **Rotisserie chicken or cooked chicken pieces** – A lifesaver when you want to add protein to a meal such as soup or fried rice but don't have to time to cook a chicken. See my Rotisserie chicken burritos (see page 83), Chicken salsa bake (see page 79), Chicken fried rice (see page 88), Chicken pot pie soup (see page 72) and Tom kha gai (see page 80).

- **Shredded ham hock** – A great addition to a pie, risotto or pasta. I even add it to savoury pancakes. See my Baked ham and pea risotto on page 157 and my Savoury pancakes on page 185.

- **Cooked salmon/mackerel/prawns (shrimp)** – Honey-roasted or sweet chilli salmon, garlic and coriander (cilantro) prawns, smoked peppered mackerel all make great additions to salads and pasta.

- **Cured meats** – Salami, chorizo, prosciutto, ham and other types of cured meat are a flavourful and quick way to add oomph to pizzas, toasties, salads, pasta and risotto. Check out my Pizza toasts on page 189.

- **Ravioli** – I love to buy filled ravioli and serve it in a quick homemade sauce. Pesto, creamy lemon, tomato and chilli and garlic butter sauce are my favourites. Cook the ravioli according to the packet instructions and toss them in your favourite sauce. You could add spinach, peppers, peas, mushrooms, Parmesan, chilli (red pepper) flakes etc to add even more flavour.

- **Cooked noodles** – Add these into soups and stir-fries for a filling addition that only takes a minute or two.

- **Microwave rice** – This often isn't quite as good as home-cooked but is a quick and useful addition to things like burritos, salad bowls and stuffed peppers. I'll also use it if I have a leftover portion of curry or chilli, which I know will only take a few minutes to heat up.

- **Frozen mashed potato pellets** – Since I discovered mashed potato pellets a couple of years ago, I don't think I've made mashed potato since! I admit, I used to feel like it was cheating at first, but now I rave about them to everyone. They usually have a good (small) ingredients list – potato, milk, butter, salt and pepper. I use them as regular mash (with extra butter and cream), to top fish pies and cottage/shepherd's pies, to make fishcakes, croquettes and even gnocchi. I *always* have some in my freezer.

- **Chips/wedges/roast potatoes** – I love homemade chips and crispy potatoes, but it's always useful to have these on standby in the freezer to whip up a quick dinner. Steaky chips (chips covered with strips of steak and peppercorn sauce, see page 108), pizza-loaded chips, as a side dish to crispy chicken or good ol' fish fingers are my favourite ways to use them.

- **Frozen vegetables** – Frozen peas are always in my freezer. They're a great addition to lots of meals, but also my favourite standby when I've run out of fresh veg. Frozen ready-chopped onions are also a brilliant time-saver (no onion-chopping tears either!).

I particularly like frozen spinach too. While it doesn't save any time (compared to using fresh spinach) it lasts for so much longer in the freezer. I hate finding a bag of slimy spinach in the refrigerator! Added to curries and sauces, you can barely tell the difference between fresh and frozen.

Other frozen vegetables, such as carrots, cauliflower, broccoli and green beans, I use a little more sparingly, as I find they don't have quite as much flavour as fresh, and they can sometimes be a little on the mushy side, but they work really well added to soups and stews. It can be a cost-effective way to buy vegetables, they're often just as nutritious as fresh vegetables and they're great to have on standby.

- **Ready-grated (pre-shredded) cheese** – Useful to speed up things and prevent accidentally grating your knuckles (I've done that a few times), however, it is more expensive than block cheese. I find the milder ones can be tasteless, so I'd always go for a stronger/mature (sharp) grated cheese if possible. Also, note that ready-grated cheese is often mixed with some kind of flour/starch to stop it sticking together. This can sometimes make it taste a little powdery if you're not cooking/melting it.

- **Sauces** – I do like making homemade sauces and I often find them more flavourful (with far fewer additives) than store-bought. If you're already cooking meat, vegetables, pasta etc, then it's usually no quicker to use a jar of pasta sauce or curry sauce than it is to make your own while you're cooking everything else. So, I don't tend to buy jars of curry or pasta sauce. I've got a number of make-ahead sauces in the Super sauces chapter (see pages 190–205). That said, jars of curry paste are very useful as they are usually flavourful and they're an easy and quick replacement for lots of spices that you would have to use if you're making your own.

Other sauces that I like to have in for when I'm short on time include pesto (fresh pesto from the refrigerator aisle is usually more vibrant and flavourful than jarred pesto, but has a much shorter shelf-life) and custard (literally one minute to heat up a pot of custard. I use store-bought custard far more often than making my own).

- **Stock** – Stock (bouillon) pots/cubes or ready-made stock are a must for adding flavour to sauces, stews, curries etc. I always have stock cubes in my cupboard to crumble directly into dishes for added flavour. I use stock cubes or liquid stock concentrate for making up quick liquid stock for gravies and sauces.

- **Pastry** – A freezer-essential for making sweet and savoury pies, pasties and sausage rolls. I will sometimes make my own if I have lots of time, but more often than not, I buy pastry. It's very easy to use (especially ready-rolled pastry), tastes great and lasts for ages in the freezer.

- **Garlic/ginger/lemongrass paste** – While I usually have all three in the refrigerator, I find that ginger and lemongrass paste have the best, truest flavour (closest to fresh versions). Garlic paste usually doesn't taste as good as freshly minced garlic, so I only use garlic paste in dishes where the garlic flavour is less prominent.

Make-ahead at home ingredients

You might think of this as the 'meal prep' you see on social media, where people make lunches or dinners ahead and box them up for the week ahead, but for me this is more about making parts of a recipe in advance, so it's quicker to pull it all together come mealtime. It's not about spending hours in the kitchen, prepping lots of ingredients, this is mostly about little extras you can add to the refrigerator and freezer when you're doing other things, recipe prep that is fairly hands-off.

Cooked rice – Microwave rice is fine at a pinch, but a cheaper and tastier alternative is to prep your own. Cook a large batch of rice ahead of time, then spread it out on a tray to quickly cool, then bag up in portions and freeze. You can defrost overnight in the refrigerator or defrost in the microwave. Reheat in the microwave or fry it up in a wok.

There are a few rules to follow when saving rice:

- Don't leave cooked rice out at room temperature. Bacteria can grow on cooked rice very quickly, so it's important to refrigerate it as quickly as possible once cooled.
- Don't store for more than 24 hours in the refrigerator.
- Thoroughly reheat it.
- Don't reheat it more than once.

Stock – Homemade stock always has the best flavour, but it takes time to make. I use stock (bouillon) cubes for stock nine times out of ten, but homemade stock makes a delicious addition to soups, sauces and gravies.

Whenever you roast meat on the bone, save the bone/carcass and freeze it. When you have a few saved up, put them in a large pan with lots of water and a few roughly chopped pieces of vegetable (onion, carrot, celery add good flavour). Simmer for up to 6 hours or until the liquid has reduced by three-quarters.

The longer you cook, the more flavour you'll get, so you can top up with more water if it's evaporating too quickly. If you want even more flavour, add a couple of stock cubes to the simmering liquid.

Strain, allow to cool and store in the refrigerator for up to two days, or freeze in portions. Then add to soups, sauces and gravies when needed.

Breadcrumbs – Got bread that's starting to look a little dry? Grate (shred) the bread or use a food processor to reduce it to crumbs, then place in a freezer bag and freeze. You can grab a handful to use (no need to thaw) whenever you'd normally use panko or fresh breadcrumbs.

Salad dressing – Make up a batch of base salad dressing by whisking together 240ml (1 cup) olive oil, ½ teaspoon each of salt and pepper, plus the juice of 1 lemon (or 2 tablespoons of red or white wine vinegar or cider vinegar). Store in a sealed jar, in the refrigerator, where it should last at least 2–3 weeks.

You can use as and when needed, as it is, or you can take out a portion and add additional ingredients for different salad dressings. Extra flavours you could add include:

- Honey
- Mustard (Dijon or wholegrain make nice additions)
- Hot sauce (sriracha, sweet chilli or hot pepper sauce)
- Dried or finely chopped fresh herbs, such as parsley, oregano, mint, coriander (cilantro), chives, dill or thyme
- Spices or aromatics, such as smoked paprika, garlic powder, cayenne pepper, minced garlic, lemongrass paste, ginger (fresh, paste or dried)

Cheese – Grate (shred) a block of cheese (or use the grater attachment on a food processor if you have one) and refrigerate in an airtight container, so you have grated cheese whenever you need it. Although you can buy ready-grated (pre-shredded) cheese, home-grated cheese is tastier, cheaper and doesn't have the extra additives

Dessert – Although this book is about quick dinner recipes I couldn't not talk a tiny bit about dessert!

Crumble topping – If you're making a fruit crumble, make double the amount of crumble topping and freeze half of it (uncooked). Having ready-made topping in the freezer means you can have a crumble prepped and ready to go in the oven in 5 minutes.

For the fruit part of the crumble, use fruit that doesn't need to be peeled and chopped, such as blueberries, blackberries or raspberries, with a sprinkling of sugar.

Stewed fruit – If you have fruit that's starting to look a little overripe (such as apples, pears, berries, rhubarb and plums), peel, core or stone before chopping and then cook them in a pan with a splash of water and a sprinkling of sugar until soft. Then cool, place in a freezerproof container and freeze.

Defrost in the refrigerator overnight, then reheat and serve with cream or custard for an easy dessert or use as a quick pie or crumble filling.

Quicker than your usual

These are time-saving swaps I make when I know I'm going to be in a real hurry:

- **Rice for couscous** – Hands up, this isn't a perfect swap and doesn't work for everything (chicken fried couscous doesn't have the same ring to it LOL!), but couscous does go well with chilli con carne, burrito bowls and stuffed peppers. Plus, it only takes a few minutes to cook.

- **Pizza dough** – Of course you can buy a ready-made pizza, but if you want to make your own, without spending time preparing and proving dough, then store-bought dough is useful. I find that chilled or frozen and defrosted pizza dough (that you roll out yourself) is much tastier than ready-made par-cooked pizza bases.

  You could also swap out the pizza base for store-bought fluffy naan or Greek flatbreads for a flavourful alternative. See my Naan chicken tikka pizza on page 64.

- **Dried pasta for fresh pasta** – Fresh pasta is more expensive than dried pasta, but it usually only takes a couple of minutes to cook in salted boiling water – making it a great time saver. Fresh pasta drizzled with a little extra virgin olive oil and sprinkled with a pinch of salt and chilli (red pepper) flakes is one of my favourite 5-minute dinners.

- **Dried beans and pulses for canned/sachets of cooked beans and pulses** – Canned beans/pulses (baked beans, kidney beans, chickpeas etc) are a fairly obvious swap and very readily available, but have you tried sachets of cooked lentils or quinoa? You can get unflavoured or flavoured versions and serve them hot or cold. They make a lovely addition to soups, salads, buddha bowls etc.

  Canned butter (lima) beans are also one of my favourite quick additions to curries and soups. They also taste delicious, mashed up with a little butter and seasoning for a side dish or dip.

Batch cooking: storage and reheating

I'm a big fan of doubling up recipes and freezing half to use for a future meal, as that means that next time I can just grab something from the freezer (like the Quick chilli con carne on page 112 and some rice) and we can have a dinner on the table in minutes!

The recipes that tend to lend themselves well to cooking then freezing are those with lots of sauce and sliced, shredded, minced or ground meat recipes. Pasta- or rice-based recipes can also work, although they tend to absorb more liquid as they cool, so they'll soften a little.

Recipes that don't work so well when cooking ahead and freezing include ones with whole fillets or big chunks of fish (they tend to dry out and overcook too easily), those with low-fat dairy (the sauce is prone to splitting) and dishes that contain ingredients with a high water content, such as stir-fries with lots of vegetables (the water in them crystallizes, resulting in a mushy texture upon reheating).

If you are freezing meals, it's always important to cool them as quickly as possible after cooking, then freeze in an airtight container. Don't forget to clearly label and date them too – so you know for how long the food has been frozen and you can easily identify what it is before defrosting in the refrigerator. Remember to reheat until piping hot throughout.

For many dishes, you likely need to reheat covered (with a lid, if in a pan, or with foil in the oven) and add a splash of water or stock to help loosen everything up and prevent the food from drying out.

My favourite recipes to batch cook include:

- Bolognese (see page 204)
- Tomato ragù (see page 192)
- Chilli con carne (see page 112)
- Casseroles
- Soups
- Stews
- Sweet and savoury pie fillings

You can freeze these types of recipes in individual or family-sized portions. Then defrost overnight in the refrigerator and reheat the following day.

Clever leftovers

If you've got room in your freezer, saving leftovers can be a lifesaver on busy weeknights. Even if there's just one portion left, freeze it! These small portions can be used for a future lunch, or one of our favourite ways to use them is to have a mix-and-match buffet, pulling out the leftovers that work together to form a meal with lots of different bits to pick from.

The best types of leftovers for freezing include:

- Cooked, shredded meat
- Roast potatoes/wedges
- Stuffing
- Yorkshire puddings
- Gravy
- Roasted chunks of vegetables
- Curry
- Pasta with sauce (or just the sauce)
- Meatballs
- Chilli con carne
- Cooked rice
- Soup
- Also, don't forget to freeze those leftover bones to make into stock (see page 8). Cool them quickly, place in an airtight container/bag and date and label them.

Flavour hacks

When you're cooking a quick dinner, you may sometimes find that you find you're not getting as much flavour in there as you would in a dish that takes longer to cook.

Consider the following:
- Taking time to sweat down onions and other vegetables adds sweetness and complexity to a dish.
- Roasting meats and vegetables until they're tender and browned makes them richer and tastier. This is due to the Maillard reaction– a chemical reaction between amino acids and reducing sugars when food is heated which results in browning.
- Allowing sauces, soups and stews to reduce makes the dish more flavourful. This is because the flavours are concentrated as water evaporates off during simmering. Sauces thicken and flavours develop further over a longer cooking period.

With all this in mind, I'm always looking for ways to make food that's cooked quickly, taste better. What hacks can I use to make up for the missing elements you would get when you're cooking a dish for longer?

I like to go back to the basics of what makes savoury food taste good.

Think back to some of your most enjoyable meals. My guess is that most, if not all, will have an element of fattiness, saltiness and acidity. These three elements are what make savoury food tasty and satisfying. There may also be a fourth element – sweetness – that helps to enhance the flavour further.

Getting the balance right on these elements can really help to elevate a meal. So, if you're cooking a quick dinner and you're worried it's lacking in flavour, have a taste, close your eyes and ask yourself if adding (or increasing) one or more of these elements would improve the flavour. Now, what can you add that will supply that required element, while also complementing the existing flavour of the dish?

Fats
- A knob of butter
- A dash of olive oil, sesame oil or chilli oil
- Cream, yogurt or crème fraîche
- A sprinkling of cheese (maybe melt in a little finely grated Cheddar or Parmesan – this will add saltiness too)

Salt
- Sea salt, flavoured salt
- Stock (or crumbled stock [bouillon] cube)
- Soy sauce
- Miso paste
- Marmite®
- Finely chopped capers/anchovies/pickles
- Crumbled bacon

Acids
- Lemon or lime juice
- Vinegars – red/white wine vinegar, cider vinegar, balsamic, malt vinegar, rice wine vinegar
- Hot pepper sauce (often quite 'vinegary')
- Worcestershire sauce
- Pickle juice (I love adding a little juice from pickled red cabbage to stews and gravy)
- Dry wines
- Tomato ketchup (also adds sweetness and saltiness)

Sweetness
- Sugar – white, light brown or dark brown
- Honey
- Golden syrup
- Molasses

In the recipes in this book I'm using a lot of these flavour hacks so you don't have to think about it but don't be afraid of tasting the dish you're cooking up and adding a little sweetness, acidity, salt or fat to boost the flavour. Just make sure you taste it first, then add a little at a time, you can always add more but you can't take it away.

One pot

One-pot, one-pan, one-dish meals can often be a time-saver in terms of hands-on cooking time, but crucially, they're also a time-saver when it comes to cleaning up!

Some people aren't as keen on one-pot cooking, believing 'it makes everything taste the same'.

The best way to get around this is to look for one-pot dishes that have a variety of textures, such as meat, vegetables and pasta or rice. Ideally, rather than just adding everything at the same time, use ingredients that require different cooking times. This will give you different textures and helps to add an element of freshness to a meal.

For example:

- **For the One-pan spaghetti and meatballs** there is a three-stage process - browning the meatballs, adding the sauce, then cooking the pasta, all in the same pan. This process gives you tender meatballs, flavourful sauce (that thickens as the pasta absorbs the liquid) and perfect al dente pasta. See my recipe on page 138.

- **More one-pan** recipes in this book include One-pan chicken and broccoli pasta (see page 122) and One-pan minced beef macaroni (see page 142).

If you do prefer to add everything to the pan or tray all at once, it can be a good idea to serve with something of a different texture. For example, the ingredients for my Chicken and chilli sauce traybake (see page 68) are all added at the same time, but I serve it with boiled rice or noodles.

Vitally Veggie

I have to try REALLY hard to get vegetarian recipes past my lot at home, so rest assured, these recipes are flavourful and satisfying, and you really won't miss the meat!

The **Sesame cauliflower** (see page 32) is a vegetarian take on one of the most popular recipes on my website – sesame chicken. It's so good that an extra-large cauliflower is devoured within minutes of it being dished up. When does that ever happen?!

I absolutely adore the **Spicy fried eggs** (see page 28) complete with crispy edges, crunchy onions and blobs of creamy, garlicky yogurt that are perfect for dunking some warmed pitta into.

And yes, I may have gone a little mushroom crazy, with THREE mushroom-based recipes in this section, but I just couldn't choose one to leave out. They're all equally delicious!

Creamy mushroom pasta

A rich and comforting meat-free dinner of creamy pasta with lots of mushrooms. The sauce is luscious and thick, and it clings to the pasta beautifully. It's ready in 15 minutes, so it makes a great weeknight dinner when you need food on the table fast!

 Serves 4   **Prep time** 5 mins   **Cook time** 10 mins   **Total time** 15 mins

300g (10½oz) tagliatelle or fettuccine

3 tablespoons unsalted butter

1 tablespoon oil

1 small onion, peeled and chopped finely

400g (14oz) chestnut (cremini) mushrooms, thickly sliced

3 garlic cloves, peeled and minced

½ teaspoon salt

½ teaspoon ground black pepper, plus extra to serve

180ml (¾ cup) vegetable stock (or chicken stock for non-vegetarians)

180ml (¾ cup) double (heavy) cream

50g (½ cup) grated (shredded) vegetarian Italian-style hard cheese (use Parmesan for non-vegetarians if preferred), plus extra to serve

To serve

a small bunch of fresh curly parsley, finely chopped

1 Cook the pasta in boiling salted water, as per the packet instructions, then drain, reserving a cup of the cooking water.

2 While the pasta is cooking, add 1 tablespoon of the butter and the oil to a frying pan (skillet) over a medium heat.

3 When the butter has melted, add the onion. Cook for 2–3 minutes, stirring often, until the onion is just starting to soften.

4 Add the remaining 2 tablespoons of butter to the pan and melt. Add the mushrooms, garlic, salt and pepper and cook for 3 minutes, stirring often, until lightly softened.

5 Stir in the stock and cream and bring to the boil. Simmer gently for 3 minutes until slightly thickened.

6 By now your pasta should be ready. Add the pasta to the pan, then sprinkle over the cheese. Use a set of tongs to lift and drop the pasta in the mushroom sauce until the pasta is fully coated in the sauce.

7 If you want to loosen up the sauce a little, add in splashes of the reserved pasta cooking water until the sauce consistency is to your liking.

8 Divide between bowls and top with chopped parsley and an extra sprinkling of black pepper and grated cheese.

Nicky's pro tips

Replace the cream with crème fraîche for a lighter version. If you're using a lower-fat version, just heat it through gently, as low-fat dairy will often split over high heat (full-fat crème fraîche can be boiled and simmered with no risk of splitting).

Vegetarian sausage & bean one pot

£

This is a lovely, warming, comforting dinner, all made in one pot. I use canned potatoes in this dish to speed things up (a brilliant store-cupboard staple), but you can replace with fresh potatoes you've boiled and drained if you have the time.

 Serves 4   **Prep time** 5 mins   **Cook time** 25 mins   **Total time** 30 mins

2 tablespoons oil
8 vegetarian sausages
1 x 540g (1lb 4oz) can potatoes, drained and thickly sliced
1 onion, peeled and sliced
3 garlic cloves, peeled and minced
2 teaspoons smoked paprika
1 teaspoon ground cumin
¼ teaspoon salt
¼ teaspoon ground black pepper
2 tablespoons tomato purée (paste)
1 x 400g (14oz) can finely chopped tomatoes
1 x 400g (14oz) can baked beans
120ml (½ cup) vegetable stock
2 teaspoons Dijon mustard
1 teaspoon light brown sugar

To serve
2 tablespoons chopped fresh flat-leaf parsley
1 teaspoon chilli (red pepper) flakes (optional)
crusty bread

1. Heat the oil in a large frying pan (skillet) or casserole dish over a medium-high heat. Add the sausages and cook for 7–8 minutes, turning often, until browned. Remove the sausages from the pan and place on a plate.

2. Add the potatoes, onion, garlic, paprika, cumin, salt, pepper and tomato purée to the pan. Cook for 3 minutes, stirring often.

3. Add the canned tomatoes, beans, stock, mustard and sugar. Stir together and bring to the boil.

4. Place the sausages back in the pan, reduce the heat and simmer for 10 minutes, stirring occasionally.

5. Serve topped with chopped parsley and chilli flakes and chunks of crusty bread for dipping.

Nicky's pro tips

Make it a cheesy version by stirring in 50g (½ packed cup) of grated mature (sharp) Cheddar after the sausages have simmered for 10 minutes, then sprinkling with a little more Cheddar before serving.

Vitally Veggie

£

Saucy roasted vegetable pasta with Lancashire cheese

I love the tangy Lancashire cheese in this dish; it complements the creamy vegetable sauce so well. If you can't get hold of Lancashire then Wensleydale, Cheshire or any light, tangy, crumbly cheese (such as feta) will also work well.

 Serves 4   Prep time 10 mins   Cook time 20 mins   Total time 30 mins

1 red (bell) pepper, deseeded and sliced into chunky pieces

1 yellow (bell) pepper, deseeded and sliced into chunky pieces

12 cherry tomatoes, sliced in half

1 red onion, peeled and sliced into 12 wedges

1 small courgette (zucchini), chopped into small chunks

3 tablespoons olive oil

½ teaspoon salt

½ teaspoon ground black pepper, plus extra to serve

1 teaspoon smoked paprika

1 vegetable stock cube, crumbled

1 tablespoon dried Italian herb mix

2 garlic cloves, peeled and minced

250g (9oz) fusilli (or your favourite pasta shape)

4 tablespoons double (heavy) cream

100g (3½oz) Lancashire cheese, crumbled (check it's vegetarian, if required, many are, but not all)

fresh basil leaves, to serve

1. Preheat the oven to 190°C fan/410°F/gas mark 6½.

2. Place the chopped peppers, tomatoes, red onion, courgette, oil, salt, black pepper, paprika, stock cube, Italian herb mix and garlic in a large baking tray. Toss together to coat everything in the oil and seasoning, then roast in the oven for 20 minutes, stirring once or twice during cooking, until the vegetables are tender and lightly charred.

3. Meanwhile, cook the pasta in boiling salted water, as per the packet instructions. Once cooked, drain and reserve a cup of the cooking water.

4. Remove the roasted vegetables from the oven and add the cooked pasta, cream and a good splash of the reserved pasta cooking water. Stir together to evenly distribute the pasta, vegetables and sauce. Add more cooking water if you want it a little saucier.

5. Sprinkle the crumbled cheese all over the top of the dish, then serve, topped with fresh basil leaves and a sprinkle of black pepper.

Nicky's pro tips

This dish also works well cold as a tasty pasta salad. Simply cool any leftovers, then cover and place in the refrigerator. I like to throw in some chopped lettuce and cucumber for an easy and quick lunch the next day.

Red pepper pesto pasta with feta

££

This recipe uses my simple red pepper pesto, but you can replace it with store-bought red pepper pesto or regular basil pesto if you prefer (if you're a vegetarian, remember to check the label to ensure it's a vegetarian pesto).

 Serves 4   **Prep time** 10 mins   **Cook time** 15 mins   **Total time** 25 mins

400g (14oz) rigatoni (or your favourite pasta shape)
½ batch Red pepper pesto (page 196), made with vegetarian Italian-style hard cheese
100g (3½oz) feta, crumbled
2 tablespoon pine nuts
a small handful of fresh basil leaves
ground black pepper, to taste

1 Cook the pasta in boiling salted water, as per the packet instructions.

2 While the pasta is cooking, make the red pepper pesto.

3 Once the pasta is cooked, drain, reserving a cup of the pasta cooking water.

4 Place the cooked pasta back in the pan. Add the red pepper pesto and a splash of the pasta cooking water. Stir together until the pesto coats the pasta. Add more pasta water if needed, to get the sauce consistency you want.

5 Divide the pasta between bowls and top with the crumbled feta, pine nuts, basil leaves and a good pinch of black pepper. Serve.

Nicky's pro tips

If you want to toast your pine nuts for extra flavour, place them in a dry frying pan (skillet) over a medium-high heat for a couple of minutes, stirring regularly, until browned. Keep a close eye on them, as they can burn quickly.

Vitally Veggie

Mushroom stroganoff

£

There's no need for meat when you have a giant pile of mushrooms, cooked in butter, salt and pepper. The savoury 'nuttiness' of the chestnut mushrooms, along with the creaminess and slight tang of the sauce makes this 20-minute dinner feel extravagant.

 Serves 4

 Prep time 5 mins

 Cook time 15 mins

 Total time 20 mins

1 tablespoon olive oil
2 tablespoons unsalted butter
1 onion, peeled and finely sliced
400g (14oz) chestnut (cremini) mushrooms, thickly sliced
¼ teaspoon salt
¼ teaspoon ground black pepper
2 garlic cloves, peeled and minced
240ml (1 cup) double (heavy) cream
150ml (⅔ cup) sour cream
1 tablespoon vegetarian Worcestershire sauce (or a regular version for non-vegetarians)

To serve
cooked pasta or rice – basmati and wild rice mix works particularly well with this dish
¼ teaspoon paprika
chopped fresh flat-leaf parsley

1   Heat the oil and butter in a large frying pan (skillet) over a medium–high heat until the butter starts to foam.

2   Add the onion and cook for 5 minutes, stirring often, until it starts to soften.

3   Add the mushrooms, salt and pepper and cook for a further 5 minutes, stirring often, until browned.

4   Reduce the heat to medium and stir in the garlic. Cook for a further minute, stirring.

5   Pour in the cream, followed by the sour cream and Worcestershire sauce. Stir and slowly heat through until the sauce is hot and the sauce at the edges of the pan is just starting to bubble slightly (don't let it boil). Turn off the heat.

6   Spoon the stroganoff over cooked pasta or rice and sprinkle on the paprika and parsley before serving.

Nicky's pro tips

Don't use low-fat cream for this dish. Cream with less than 25% fat can curdle when heated.

Although we're using sour cream, which is about 20% fat for the full-fat version, it is protected by the addition of the double (heavy) cream, which is about 48% fat. Ensure you pour the double cream into the hot pan before the sour cream, then heat it slowly and the sauce will be perfect.

Ravioli in garlic lemon sauce

££

This is one of my favourite ways to seriously up the game on ready-made ravioli. There's no need to boil the ravioli separately, as it cooks in the sauce, so it makes a really quick meal, which only uses one pan.

 Serves 4   Prep time 5 mins   Cook time 15 mins   Total time 20 mins

2 tablespoons olive oil

3 garlic cloves, peeled and very finely sliced (or minced if you prefer)

¼ teaspoon salt

¼ teaspoon ground black pepper, plus extra to serve

500g (1lb 2oz) fresh ravioli

60ml (¼ cup) white wine

240ml (1 cup) vegetable stock

2 tablespoons fresh lemon juice (juice of about 1 lemon)

4 tablespoons double (heavy) cream

50g (½ cup) finely grated (shredded) vegetarian Italian-style hard cheese (or use Parmesan for non-vegetarians), plus extra to serve

65g (2 cups) mild rocket (arugula)

1 Heat the oil in a large frying pan (skillet) over a low heat. Add the garlic, salt and pepper and gently sauté for 4–5 minutes until the garlic softens.

2 Stir in the fresh ravioli, then increase the heat to medium–high.

3 Add the wine and let it bubble for 1 minute, then add the stock and lemon juice. Stir together and simmer for 3–4 minutes, stirring occasionally.

4 Carefully stir in the cream and cheese and cook for a further 1–2 minutes, stirring often, until the ravioli is piping hot throughout (you can check this by slicing into one of the pieces of ravioli).

5 Turn off the heat and stir in the rocket – it should wilt slightly.

6 Divide between bowls and top with black pepper and a little more finely grated cheese.

Nicky's pro tips

Use your favourite fresh ravioli for this recipe. I think it works particularly well using ravioli filled with spinach and ricotta, porcini mushrooms or butternut squash.

Vitally Veggie

Spicy fried eggs with garlic & chilli oil

This recipe started out as a take on Turkish eggs, which I've adapted over time. It's really easy to throw together and it's what I make when I'm craving something quick and spicy. I love to dip toasted flatbreads or warmed pitta into the runny eggs yolks and yogurt, then spoon on some of the salty-spicy spring onions and crispy onions.

 Serves 2   **Prep time** 5 mins   **Cook time** 6 mins   **Total time** 11 mins

2 tablespoons oil

4 medium eggs

4 spring onions (scallions), finely sliced

2 garlic cloves, peeled and minced

1 red chilli, sliced

¼ teaspoon white pepper

1 tablespoon light soy sauce

2 tablespoons oyster sauce

4 tablespoons thick natural yogurt

3 tablespoons crispy fried onions (see Tip)

To serve

1 tablespoon chilli oil

½ teaspoon chilli (red pepper) flakes

1 tablespoon sesame seeds

boiled rice or toasted flatbreads (optional)

1   Heat the oil in a large frying pan (skillet) over a medium–high heat.

2   When the oil is hot, carefully crack the eggs into the pan, so they're evenly spaced, with a gap between each egg. Cook for 2 minutes until the whites are cooked at the edges, but not quite done near the yolk.

3   Reduce the heat to medium. Scatter the spring onions garlic, chilli and white pepper in the spaces between the eggs and use a spatula to move them around a little for 1 minute.

4   Mix together the soy sauce, oyster sauce and 2 tablespoons of water. Pour over the spring onions and stir the sauce into the spring onions.

5   Add four blobs of yogurt into the pan and swirl into the spring onions slightly, but don't mix it in completely. We want four separate areas of yogurt.

6   Cook for another minute until the yogurt is slightly warmed through (it doesn't need to be hot), the spring onions are tender and the egg whites are cooked (the yolks should still be runny).

7   Turn off the heat and sprinkle on the crispy onions.

8   Serve the eggs topped with a drizzle of chilli oil and a sprinkling of chilli flakes and sesame seeds. You can eat them on their own, or serve over rice, or with flatbreads for dipping in the eggs and yogurt.

Nicky's pro tips

You can buy crispy fried onions in little tubs at most supermarkets. They're usually with the salad dressings/toppers and/or the world food section.

Cheddar & vegetable chowder

££

A simple, creamy-cheesy soup served in a bread bowl. I've never been able to finish the bread bowl yet, but I'll keep practising! This recipe uses frozen vegetables, but you could replace with canned (drained) vegetables or fresh vegetables if you prefer.

 Serves
4

 Prep time
5 mins

 Cook time
20 mins

 Total time
25 mins

2 tablespoons unsalted butter

3 tablespoons plain (all-purpose) flour

1 litre (4 cups + 3 tablespoons) full-fat (whole) milk

2 teaspoons vegetable bouillon or 2 vegetable stock (bouillon) cubes, crumbled

½ teaspoon salt

½ teaspoon ground black pepper

500g (1lb 2oz) mixed frozen vegetables

100g (1 packed cup) grated (shredded) mature (sharp) Cheddar, plus 25g (¼ packed cup) to serve

4 large bread cobs, to serve

1 Place a large saucepan over a medium heat. Add the butter and allow to melt.

2 Once melted, add the flour and stir using a whisk for 1 minute. Slowly pour in the milk, while stirring with the whisk, until all the milk is added.

3 Continue to heat, while stirring, until the sauce thickens (this will happen as it approaches boiling point). This should take about 5 minutes.

4 Add the vegetable bouillon, salt, pepper and frozen vegetables. Stir together, bring to a simmer and allow it to bubble gently for 6–8 minutes until the vegetables are tender.

5 Stir in the cheese and reduce the heat to low.

6 Take the bread cobs and slice off the tops. Scoop out most of the bread inside to form bread bowls (be careful not to tear the outside of the bread bowls).

7 Place the bread bowls on plates. Turn off the heat for the chowder and ladle the chowder into the bread bowls.

8 Sprinkle over the cheese and serve.

🗨️ Nicky's pro tips

If you want to use fresh vegetables, be sure to cut them into small cubes/pieces. Quicker cook vegetables such as cauliflower, broccoli and green beans work well and can be added directly to the sauce (as you would the frozen vegetables). If you want to use root vegetables, such as carrots and/or potatoes, cut into small dice then steam or boil for 6–8 minutes before adding to the sauce.

Vitally Veggie

Sesame cauliflower

This sesame cauliflower is a vegetarian take on one of the most popular recipes on my website – sesame chicken. I find cauliflower makes a great alternative due to the tender texture when stir-fried. We're frying the cauliflower first to give it a slight charred flavour, then it's cooked for a few minutes in stock and the rest of the sauce ingredients, to make it tender, but with a bit of crunch. I like to serve it topped with plenty of sesame seeds and lots of fluffy boiled rice.

 Serves 4

 Prep time 10 mins

 Cook time 15 mins

 Total time 25 mins

600–650g (1lb 5oz–1lb 7oz) cauliflower florets (about 1 extra-large cauliflower)
2 tablespoons sesame oil
a pinch of salt and pepper
120ml (½ cup) vegetable stock
3 garlic cloves, peeled and minced
1 tablespoon white wine vinegar
2 tablespoons honey
2 tablespoons sweet chilli sauce
3 tablespoons tomato ketchup
2 tablespoons light brown sugar
2 tablespoons dark soy sauce
½ tablespoon cornflour (cornstarch), mixed with 2 tablespoons cold water to form a slurry

To serve
boiled or fried rice
2 teaspoons mixed black and white sesame seeds
2 spring onions (scallions), sliced

1   Break the cauliflower florets into bite-size pieces.

2   Heat the sesame oil in a wok over a medium heat. When hot, add the cauliflower, salt and pepper. Stir-fry for 5 minutes until the cauliflower is starting to brown at the edges.

3   Add the stock, increase the heat to high and continue to cook the cauliflower in the bubbling stock, tossing it together regularly, for 3 minutes.

4   Add the garlic, vinegar, honey, sweet chilli sauce, ketchup, sugar and soy sauce and stir together. Bring to the boil, reduce the heat to medium and allow the mixture to simmer, stirring often, for 5 minutes.

5   Move the cauliflower over to one side of the wok and stir in the cornflour slurry to thicken the sauce. Cook for another minute, then turn off the heat.

6   Serve the sesame cauliflower with rice, topped with sesame seeds and spring onions.

Nicky's pro tips

Add more vegetables to this dish if you like – broccoli and mushrooms are great additions that take a similar amount of time to cook as the cauliflower.

Spicy egg curry

A fragrant, tangy and slightly creamy curry. I use six eggs for four people,
so everyone gets three halves each, but you can add more if you prefer.

 Serves 4   **Prep time** 10 mins   **Cook time** 20 mins   **Total time** 30 mins

6 medium eggs, at room
   temperature
2 tablespoons oil or ghee
1 large onion, peeled and thickly
   sliced
1 red chilli, sliced
1 green chilli, sliced
2 garlic cloves, peeled and minced
2 teaspoons minced ginger
1 teaspoon garam masala
1 teaspoon ground cumin
1 teaspoon ground turmeric
2 teaspoons ground coriander
½ teaspoon ground cinnamon
1½ teaspoons salt
1 tablespoon tomato purée (paste)
1 red (bell) pepper, deseeded and
   diced
1 green (bell) pepper, deseeded
   and diced
1 x 400g (14oz) can finely
   chopped tomatoes
200ml (¾ cup + 1 tablespoon)
   coconut cream

To serve
boiled rice
chopped fresh coriander (cilantro)
chilli (red pepper) flakes
nigella seeds

1 Place the eggs in a pan of cold water. Bring to the boil, then simmer for
6–8 minutes (6 for a soft yolk, 8 for a firm yolk). Once cooked, remove
from the pan and place in a bowl of cold water with ice to cool.

2 While the eggs are cooking, start on the curry sauce. Heat the oil (or
ghee) in a large frying pan (skillet) over a medium heat.

3 Add the onion, chillies, garlic, ginger, garam masala, cumin, turmeric,
ground coriander, cinnamon, salt and tomato purée. Fry for 3 minutes,
stirring often, until the onion starts to soften.

4 Add the red and green peppers, canned tomatoes and coconut cream.
Stir together, bring to the boil, then simmer for 5–6 minutes, stirring
occasionally, until reduced slightly.

5 Meanwhile, remove the eggs from the bowl of water. Peel off the shells
and slice the eggs in half. Add the eggs to the curry and allow them to
heat through for a further 3–4 minutes.

6 Turn off the heat and divide between bowls with rice. Top with fresh
coriander, chilli flakes and nigella seeds, then serve.

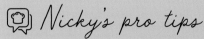

Nicky's pro tips
Roll the hard-boiled eggs on the work surface to crack the shell all
over, this will help with peeling the egg.

Vitally Veggie

Pan-fried creamy mushrooms with spinach

No-one else in my family likes mushrooms, so I make this one when I've got the house to myself! A super-quick, filling and comforting mushroom dish in a lovely creamy sauce. I like to serve it up with extra cheese and chunks of toasted bread for dipping.

 Serves 2   **Prep time** 5 mins   **Cook time** 15 mins   **Total time** 20 mins

1 tablespoon oil

1 tablespoon unsalted butter

200g (7oz) baby chestnut (cremini) mushrooms, sliced in half

1 small onion, peeled and sliced

¼ teaspoon salt

¼ teaspoon ground black pepper, plus extra to serve

2 garlic cloves, peeled and minced

½ teaspoon dried thyme

60ml (¼ cup) white wine

240ml (1 cup) vegetable stock

120ml (½ cup) double (heavy) cream

50g (½cup) grated (shredded) vegetarian Italian-style hard cheese (or Parmesan for non-vegetarians), plus extra to serve

90g (3 cups) baby spinach

To serve

fresh or dried thyme leaves

thick slices of bread, toasted

1 Heat the oil and butter in a large frying pan (skillet) over a medium–high heat.

2 When the butter has melted, add the mushrooms, onion, salt and pepper. Fry for 5–6 minutes until the mushrooms are browned.

3 Add the garlic and thyme and stir, then pour in the white wine. Allow to bubble for 1 minute, then add the stock. Bring to the boil and simmer for 5 minutes until slightly reduced.

4 Stir in the cream, cheese and spinach. Heat through for 2 minutes, stirring, until the spinach has wilted.

5 Top with extra cheese, a sprinkling of black pepper and a few thyme leaves. I like to serve with chunks of toasted bread for dipping.

Nicky's pro tips

Use your favourite mushrooms for this recipe. I find chestnut mushrooms have a lovely flavour, but regular button mushrooms, sliced portobello mushrooms and oyster mushrooms all work well.

Fantastic Fish

Living near the sea, close to a busy fishing ports in the UK, fish is becoming much more of a regular occurrence on our menu at home, and that makes me so happy!

I think most people tend to default to salmon or tuna, as these have the most familiar flavours. So, of course, I've included recipes with those fish. But I've also included a couple of recipes with fish you may not have cooked with before. The **Creamy lemon butter sea bream** (see page 55) is a lovely light and flaky fish that cooks in minutes but looks impressive. Perfect for date night!

If you've never tried basa, try my **lemon feta baked basa** (see page 59), with tomatoes, capers and crumbled feta. It makes a lovely summer dinner.

The **Teriyaki salmon bites** (see page 44) are the most popular in my house. Try them as part of a rice bowl, stuffed into tacos or nestled in some sesame noodles.

Pan-fried salmon with lemon orzo

Beautifully seasoned, tender, pan-fried salmon, nestled in a bed of creamy orzo with lemon and Parmesan. It feels like a really special dinner, yet it's quick to make and all cooked in one pan (no pre-boiling of the orzo needed). I love to use orzo as an alternative to risotto for a dinner that cooks in far less time!

 Serves 4   **Prep time** 10 mins   **Cook time** 20 mins   **Total time** 30 mins

4 skin-on salmon fillets
a pinch of salt
a pinch of garlic salt
¼ teaspoon ground black pepper, plus extra to serve
⅛ teaspoon paprika
½ teaspoon dried parsley
2 tablespoons olive oil
2 tablespoons unsalted butter

Orzo

2 garlic cloves, peeled and minced
230g (1 cup plus 2 tablespoons) orzo
480ml (2 cups) chicken stock
60ml (¼ cup) double (heavy) cream
75g (¾ cup) grated (shredded) Parmesan
zest and juice of ½ lemon
¼ teaspoon salt
½ teaspoon ground black pepper

To serve

a small bunch of fresh flat-leaf parsley, finely chopped
lemon wedges

1   Place the salmon fillets on a plate skin-side down. Mix together the salt, garlic salt, pepper, paprika and dried parsley. Sprinkle onto the top of the salmon and pat it down, so it sticks.

2   Heat the oil and butter in a large frying pan (skillet), over a medium–high heat.

3   Add the salmon fillets, skin-side up (so the part coated with the spice mix is in the oil). Cook for 3–4 minutes until the salmon is golden brown, then remove the salmon from the pan and place on a plate, skin-side down (we'll continue cooking it shortly).

4   Reduce the heat to medium and add the garlic to the pan. Cook for 30 seconds, stirring constantly, so the garlic doesn't burn.

5   Add the orzo to the pan, stir with the garlic, then add the chicken stock and stir again.

6   Nestle the salmon fillets into the orzo, skin-side down. Increase the heat to medium–high and bring to the boil, then reduce the heat and simmer for 8–9 minutes, stirring occasionally, until the orzo is al dente (cooked, but with a little bite). You'll need to move the salmon with a set of tongs to stir the orzo underneath, so it doesn't stick to the pan.

7   Add the cream, Parmesan, lemon zest and juice, salt and pepper to the orzo and stir together.

8   Turn off the heat, sprinkle on the chopped parsley and a little black pepper. Arrange the lemon wedges in the pan, then serve.

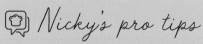 *Nicky's pro tips*

Want to add vegetables? Add frozen peas or sliced mangetout into the pan during the last 5 minutes of cooking or add trimmed and chopped fine asparagus or fine green beans at the same time as the orzo.

Glazed salmon & garlic greens

This Chinese-inspired salmon and greens dish makes a tasty lighter meal with only 10 minutes cooking time. If you wanted to bulk it out, serve with rice or noodles too. If there's any of the salmon glaze left on the grill tray after cooking, be sure to drizzle it on top – we don't want any of that lovely sauce going to waste.

 Serves 4　　 **Prep time** 10 mins　　 **Cook time** 10 mins　　 **Total time** 20 mins

---

4 tail-end, skin-on salmon fillets
　(the wider, flatter salmon fillets)
1 tablespoon oil
1 tablespoon sesame oil
1 tablespoon light soy sauce
1 tablespoon dark soy sauce
¼ teaspoon garlic powder
¼ teaspoon ground black pepper
3 tablespoons light brown sugar
1 tablespoon sesame seeds, to serve

Greens
2 tablespoons sesame oil
400g (14oz) pak choi (bok choi),
　leaves separated, rinsed and dried
a bunch of spring onions
　(scallions), trimmed
2 garlic cloves, peeled and minced
2 red chillies, sliced
2 tablespoons dark soy sauce

1　Preheat the grill (broiler) to high.

2　Place the salmon fillets, skin-side up on a grill tray lined with foil. Place under the grill for 2 minutes.

3　Meanwhile, in a small bowl, mix together the oil, sesame oil, light soy sauce, dark soy sauce, garlic powder, pepper and sugar.

4　Turn the salmon over and drizzle the glaze over the salmon (don't worry about the sauce pooling on the tray). Place under the grill and cook for a further 4–6 minutes, basting two or three times, until just cooked.

5　While the salmon is cooking, make the greens. Heat the sesame oil in a large frying pan (skillet) or wok over a medium–high heat. Add the ak choi, spring onions, garlic, chillies and soy sauce and stir-fry, tossing everything together, until the pak choi and spring onions soften (about 3–4 minutes).

6　Arrange the salmon and stir-fried greens on plates and top with sesame seeds.

Nicky's pro tips
Swap out the pak choi and spring onions for your favourite quick-cook vegetables – such as mangetout, (bell) peppers, spring greens or kale.

Fantastic Fish

Teriyaki salmon bites

For some reason my whole family loves salmon bites more than whole pieces of salmon – even when they're cooked in the same way, with the same sauce! It makes a great dinner, but also fantastic party food. Serve on sticks and they'll be gobbled up in no time!

 Serves 4 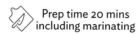 Prep time 20 mins including marinating Cook time 10 mins Total time 30 mins

4 salmon fillets (about 480g/1lb 1oz), skin removed and sliced into 2.5cm (1in) chunks
1 tablespoon oil

Teriyaki sauce
2 tablespoons light soy sauce
3 tablespoons dark soy sauce
1 tablespoon sake or dry sherry
3 tablespoons mirin
1 teaspoon sesame oil
1 tablespoon brown sugar
2 teaspoons minced ginger
3 garlic cloves, peeled and minced
½ teaspoon white pepper

To serve
2 spring onions (scallions), finely sliced
2 teaspoons black and white sesame seeds
boiled rice

1 Add all the teriyaki sauce ingredients to a bowl and mix together.

2 Place the salmon pieces in a separate bowl and add 2 tablespoons of the teriyaki sauce. Mix to coat, then cover and allow to marinate for 10 minutes.

3 Heat the oil in a large frying pan (skillet) over a medium–high heat. Add the marinated salmon pieces and cook for 3 minutes, turning a couple of times with a set of tongs.

4 Pour the rest of the teriyaki sauce into the frying pan (be careful, it will spatter a bit). Heat through, basting the salmon pieces in the sauce, for a further 2–3 minutes until the salmon pieces are cooked through.

5 Serve the salmon bites topped with spring onions and sesame seeds. I like to serve mine with some fluffy boiled rice. There should be enough sauce in the pan so you can drizzle some on your rice too.

🗨 *Nicky's pro tips*

This recipe also works well with 12–16 king prawns (jumbo shrimp) (reduce the cooking time to about 4 minutes) or bite-size chunks of monkfish (increase the cooking time to 8–10 minutes).

Salmon with spaghetti & lemon cream sauce

££

Pan-fried salmon, flaked into tender pieces and served with spaghetti and courgetti (spiralized zucchini) in a light lemon cream sauce. Mixing the spaghetti with the courgetti gives the dish an even lighter feel, plus the courgetti is barely noticeable, so my kids eat it all, no problem!

 Serves 4

 Prep time 15 mins

 Cook time 15 mins

 Total time 30 mins

250g (9oz) spaghetti

1 tablespoon olive oil

⅛ teaspoon salt

⅛ teaspoon ground black pepper, plus extra to serve

3 skin-on salmon fillets

1 small onion, peeled and chopped

2 garlic cloves, peeled and minced

2 tablespoons white wine

5 tablespoons double (heavy) cream

zest of 1 lemon, plus juice of ½ (about 1 tablespoon)

85g (1 cup) sugar snap peas (snow peas), roughly chopped

1 small courgette (zucchini), spiralized or cut into thin strips

To serve

2 tablespoons grated (shredded) Parmesan

lemon zest

lemon wedges

1. Cook the spaghetti in a large pan of boiling salted water, as per the packet instructions. While the spaghetti is cooking, heat the oil in a large frying pan (skillet) over a medium–high heat.

2. Sprinkle the salt and pepper on the flesh of the salmon fillets and place in the pan, skin-side down. Cook for 3 minutes until the skin is crispy.

3. Turn the salmon over and add the onion to the pan. Cook the salmon and onion for a further 3 minutes until the onion starts to soften. Take the salmon out of the pan and place on a chopping board.

4. Add the garlic to the onion and cook for a minute, stirring. Add the wine and let it bubble for a minute, then pour in the cream and reduce the heat to medium.

5. While the cream heats through, remove the skin from the salmon and break the salmon into rough chunks (don't worry if it's not quite cooked at this point). Add the chunks back into the pan with the lemon zest.

6. By now the spaghetti should be almost ready. Add the peas and spiralized courgette to the spaghetti for the last minute of cooking. Then drain the pasta, reserving about ½ cup of the cooking water.

7. Add the spaghetti, sugar snaps and courgette to the frying pan and toss through along with the lemon juice and a couple of splashes of the reserved pasta water.

8. Divide between bowls and top with grated Parmesan, freshly ground black pepper and a little bit of lemon zest. Serve with lemon wedges.

Nicky's pro tips

For this recipe, there is enough sauce to coat the pasta, but if you want it to be a little saucier, add in more of the reserved pasta cooking water and an extra tablespoon of cream.

Seafood laksa

This Thai-inspired seafood laksa is a great way to get a fabulous spicy noodle dish on the table quickly, using only one pan and ready in 30 minutes. If you like spicy Thai food as much as I do, then you will LOVE this!

 Serves 4   **Prep time** 10 mins   **Cook time** 20 mins   **Total time** 30 mins

200ml (¾ cup + 1 tablespoon) full-fat coconut milk

1 teaspoon fish sauce

300ml (1¼ cups) chicken or seafood stock

2 cod, haddock or any firm-fleshed white fish fillets (about 140g/5oz each), skin removed

200g (7oz) dried rice/vermicelli noodles (or 300–400g/10½–14oz ready-cooked vermicelli noodles)

12–16 raw king prawns (jumbo shrimp), peeled and deveined

200g (7oz) bean sprouts

Laksa paste

3 tablespoons oil

1 onion, peeled and chopped

4 red chillies, roughly chopped (I use Fresno but use Thai if you like really hot chillies)

2 teaspoons ginger paste

2 garlic cloves, peeled and minced

1 teaspoon lemongrass paste

1 heaped tablespoon chopped fresh coriander (cilantro) stalks (use the leaves for garnish)

1½ teaspoons ground turmeric

½ teaspoon ground cumin

½ teaspoon paprika

1 teaspoon tamarind paste

Garnish

1 teaspoon rice wine vinegar

1 teaspoon caster (superfine) sugar

1 red chilli, finely diced

1 finger-size piece of cucumber, finely diced

¼ small red onion, peeled and finely diced

1. Start with the laksa paste. Heat the oil in a large frying pan (skillet) and add the onion. Cook over a medium heat for about 5 minutes until the onion softens and starts to turn translucent.

2. Add the remaining laksa paste ingredients, stir and continue to cook for 5 minutes, stirring occasionally.

3. While the laksa paste ingredients are frying, make the garnish. Put the ingredients and the reserved coriander (cilantro) leaves in a small bowl, stir together then set aside.

4. Turn off the heat and transfer the laksa mixture to mini chopper or food processor. Blend together until it forms a paste (alternatively, you can use a stick blender to blend the ingredients into a paste directly in the pan but be careful of splashes).

5. Add the laksa paste back into the pan. Turn the heat to medium–high and add the coconut milk, fish sauce and stock. Stir together and heat through until just simmering.

6. Meanwhile, stir and cook for 4 minutes, turning a couple of times, until the fish is starting to fall apart.

7. While the fish is cooking, soak the noodles in boiling water until soft (about 3 minutes), then drain.

8. Add the prawns to the laksa, stir and cook for 1 minute. The prawns should be starting to turn pink and your fish should be cooked.

9. Finally, add the bean sprouts and cook for another minute, so they're warmed through, but still slightly crisp. Turn off the heat.

10. Divide the noodles between bowls and spoon the laksa and seafood over the top. Top each bowl with a spoonful of garnish and serve.

💬 *Nicky's pro tips*

If you don't want to make your own laksa paste, you can use store-bought (I recommend using a Malaysian, Thai or Singapore brand, rather than an own brand). They vary in strength, so read the side of the jar to work out how much you need for four portions. I would usually start with 2 heaped tablespoons. You can always add in a little more if needed.

Tuna cheese fishcakes

£

I'm using the shortcut of frozen (and defrosted) mashed potato pellets for this recipe. I cook a lot of things from scratch, but frozen mashed potato has been a game-changer for me. It tastes exactly the same, there are no hidden nasties and it saves a massive amount of effort. It works brilliantly to speed up recipes like these tuna fishcakes.

 Serves 4   **Prep time** 10 mins   **Cook time** 10 mins   **Total time** 20 mins

500g (1lb 2oz) frozen mashed potato pellets, defrosted
145g (5oz) can tuna in olive oil, drained and flaked
100g (3½oz) drained canned sweetcorn (or use frozen and defrosted sweetcorn)
2 spring onions (scallions), sliced
100g (1 packed cup) grated (shredded) mature (sharp) Cheddar
¼ teaspoon salt
¼ teaspoon ground black pepper
4 tablespoons plain (all-purpose) flour
2 medium eggs, lightly beaten
75 g (1½ cups) panko breadcrumbs
4 tablespoons oil, for frying
sea salt, to taste (optional)
buttered green vegetables, such as peas, cabbage, green beans or broccoli, to serve

1. Place the defrosted mashed potato in a large bowl. Add the tuna, sweetcorn, spring onions, cheese, salt and pepper. Stir together to combine. Form the mixture into eight patties.

2. Place the flour in a shallow bowl, the beaten egg in a second bowl and the breadcrumbs in a third bowl.

3. Dredge the fishcakes in the flour, then dip in the egg (be sure to fully coat in the egg) and finally coat in the breadcrumbs.

4. Add the oil to a large frying pan (skillet) over a medium heat. When the oil is hot, add the fishcakes and cook for 7–8 minutes, turning once, until browned all over and hot throughout.

5. Remove from the pan (add a sprinkle of sea salt if you like) and serve. I like to serve mine with buttered peas and cabbage.

🗨 Nicky's pro tips

If you like lots of tuna, you can double the amount of tuna in this recipe. For an extra special treat, try albacore tuna. It's got a lovely creamy taste and a firmer texture.

Fantastic Fish

Tuna tomato spaghetti

££

When I was very young, I was a bit of a fussy eater. I even found spaghetti bolognese too much! So, my mum used to make me an unusual concoction of spaghetti, tuna, tomato ketchup and cheese. It sounds kind of weird now and not something I would enjoy eating! But the thought of that dish still brings me comfort. This is my grown-up version, which I've adapted over the years. It makes me smile whenever I eat it.

 Serves 4   Prep time 10 mins   Cook time 20 mins   Total time 30 mins

300g (10½oz) spaghetti
2 tablespoons extra virgin olive oil
1 onion, peeled and finely diced
2 garlic cloves, peeled and minced
¼ teaspoon salt
¼ teaspoon ground black pepper, plus extra to serve
½ teaspoon chilli (red pepper) flakes
2 x 400g (14oz) cans finely chopped tomatoes
1 teaspoon sugar
2 x 145g (5oz) cans tuna in olive oil, drained and flaked
100g (3½oz) mixed olives, drained, pitted and sliced in half

To serve
50g (½ packed cup) grated (shredded) Pecorino cheese (or Parmesan)
30g (1 packed cup) baby salad leaves
1 tablespoon extra virgin olive oil

1. Cook the pasta in boiling salted water, as per the packet instructions (ideally until al dente). Once cooked, drain, reserving ½ cup of the cooking water.

2. Meanwhile, heat the oil in a large frying pan (skillet), over a medium–high heat until hot. Add the onion and cook for 5 minutes, stirring often, until softened.

3. Add the garlic, salt, pepper and chilli flakes and stir together for a further minute.

4. Add the canned tomatoes and sugar, stir and bring to the boil. Simmer for 4–5 minutes until slightly reduced.

5. Add the tuna and olives. Stir together and cook for a further 4–5 minutes, stirring gently (so as not to mush up the tuna) a few times during cooking, until the tuna is warmed through.

6. Add the cooked spaghetti and toss together. Add in splashes of the pasta cooking water if you want to loosen up the sauce further.

7. Divide between bowls and top with grated Pecorino, salad leaves, a drizzle of extra virgin olive oil and a sprinkling of pepper before serving.

Quick & Easy

Nicky's pro tips
Swap out the spaghetti for your favourite pasta shape. I sometimes like to use farfalle or pasta shells.

Creamy lemon butter sea bream

£££

I like this as a bit of a fancy date-night meal. The sauce cooks with the fish, so it all comes together quite quickly (about 10 minutes cooking time). You can also use this recipe for other fish, such as salmon, cod or haddock. If you are using one of these chunky types of fish, add an extra 5–6 minutes to the cooking time to make sure it's fully cooked through.

 Serves
2

 Prep time
5 mins

 Cook time
10 mins

 Total time
15 mins

2 skin-on sea bream fillets
1 tablespoon plain (all-purpose) flour
a pinch of salt and pepper
1 tablespoon oil

Creamy lemon butter sauce
2 tablespoons unsalted butter
2 garlic cloves, peeled and minced
60ml (¼ cup) white wine
120ml (½ cup) double (heavy) cream
2 tablespoons capers
2 tablespoons lemon juice
¼ teaspoon salt
¼ teaspoon ground black pepper
4 tablespoons (¼ cup) chopped fresh flat-leaf parsley

To serve
mashed potato
steamed peas

1   Dust the flesh side of the fish fillets with the flour, salt and pepper.

2   Heat the oil in a large frying pan (skillet) over a medium–high heat. Add the fillets, flesh-side down, and cook for 2–3 minutes until golden brown.

3   Turn the fish over, reduce the heat to medium and immediately add the butter and garlic to the pan. Stir until the butter melts, then pour in the wine. Allow the wine to bubble for 1–2 minutes until half of it has evaporated.

4   Add the cream, capers, lemon juice, salt and pepper. Stir together and heat through for 2–3 minutes, basting the fish with the liquid until the sauce is hot and the fish is cooked through.

5   Turn off the heat and stir in the parsley.

6   I like to serve this dish with buttery mashed potato and peas. The sauce sinks into the mashed potato beautifully!

🍲 Nicky's pro tips

Want the sea bream skin crisp? Score the skin of the fish a few times before cooking. Add an extra tablespoon of oil to the pan and fry skin-side down first for 2–3 minutes, then turn over and cook for a further 2–3 minutes until the fish is browned and cooked through. Transfer to a warm plate – skin-side up – then continue making the sauce in the pan. Serve the sauce alongside the fish.

Fantastic Fish

Cajun prawns with noodles

Juicy king prawns in a spicy, slightly creamy sauce with lots of noodles makes a lovely, lip-smacking dinner. Ready-cooked noodles help to speed up this recipe and mean you only need to use one pan. However, you can use dried noodles if you prefer (use your favourite kind and cook as per the packet instructions before adding to the pan).

 Serves
4

 Prep time
10 mins

 Cook time
15 mins

 Total time
25 mins

300g (10½oz) raw king prawns (jumbo shrimp), peeled and deveined
2 tablespoons Cajun spice mix
2 tablespoons oil
1 onion, peeled and diced
1 red (bell) pepper, deseeded and diced
1 red chilli, sliced
2 garlic cloves, peeled and minced
¼ teaspoon salt
¼ teaspoon ground black pepper
180ml (¾ cup) chicken stock
1 tablespoon Worcestershire sauce
1 heaped tablespoon crème fraîche
400g (14oz) ready-cooked egg noodles
2 tablespoons finely chopped fresh coriander (cilantro)
chilli (red pepper) flakes, to serve

1 Place the prawns in a bowl and sprinkle on the Cajun spice mix. Stir together and set aside.

2 Add 1 tablespoon of the oil to a large frying pan (skillet) over a high heat. Add the prawns and cook for 2–3 minutes, turning once, until the prawns are pink. Remove the prawns from the pan and place in a bowl.

3 Reduce the heat to medium and add the remaining tablespoon of oil to the pan. Add the onion, red pepper, chilli, garlic, salt and pepper and fry for 4–5 minutes, stirring often, until the onion starts to soften.

4 Add the stock, Worcestershire sauce and crème fraîche. Stir together and heat through until just starting to boil.

5 Add the noodles and heat through for 4–5 minutes, stirring often, until the noodles are hot. Then add the cooked prawns and cook for a further minute, stirring often.

6 Turn off the heat, stir through the chopped coriander and serve topped with chilli flakes.

Nicky's pro tips

Swap out the crème fraîche for 3 tablespoons of full-fat coconut milk or double (heavy cream) if you prefer.

Lemon feta baked basa

££

I love a recipe that calls for adding everything to a dish and leaving it to cook with no intervention. This simple fish dish is packed with flavour. My serving suggestions are for potatoes, rice or pasta, but I've got to admit, sometimes I don't even bother cooking a side dish and serve with a big wedge of crusty bread for dipping in the sauce instead.

 Serves 4   Prep time 10 mins   Cook time 15–20 mins   Total time 25–30 mins

200g (7oz) cherry tomatoes, sliced in half (multicoloured tomatoes add a nice splash of colour)
1 tablespoon cornflour (cornstarch)
2 garlic cloves, peeled and minced
120ml (½ cup) chicken stock
3 tablespoons finely chopped fresh flat-leaf parsley, plus extra to serve
3 tablespoons olive oil
1 lemon, thinly sliced
2 tablespoons capers, drained
200g (7oz) feta, crumbled
4 skinless, boneless basa fillets
1 teaspoon paprika
1 teaspoon dried oregano
½ teaspoon chilli (red pepper) flakes
½ teaspoon garlic powder
½ teaspoon salt
½ teaspoon ground black pepper, plus extra to serve

To serve
boiled potatoes, rice or pasta

1. Preheat the oven to 200°C fan/425°F/gas mark 7.

2. To a large baking dish, add the sliced cherry tomatoes. Sprinkle on the cornflour and toss together, to coat the tomatoes. Add the garlic, stock, parsley and 2 tablespoons of the olive oil and toss everything together.

3. Add the sliced lemon, capers and feta to the dish and place the basa fillets on top.

4. Mix together the paprika, oregano, chilli flakes, garlic powder, salt and pepper and sprinkle on the basa fillets.

5. Drizzle the fish with the remaining tablespoon of oil, then bake in the oven for 15–20 minutes until the fish is cooked through and the tomatoes are tender.

6. Serve with potatoes, rice or pasta, topped with fresh parsley and black pepper.

Nicky's pro tips
You can replace the basa with other quick-cook thin fillets of fish, such as sole, sea bream or sea bass.

Fantastic Fish

Crispy fish burgers
with mustard pickle mayo

Such a great way to get the family to eat more fish – turn it into a burger! These crispy-coated fish fillets are devoured in no time. Shallow-frying gives the coating extra golden crispness, but I've included a tip on how to oven bake them too.

 Serves 4   **Prep time** 10 mins   **Cook time** 10 mins   **Total time** 20 mins

4 small white fish fillets (haddock, pollock or cod), about 100g (3½oz) each
60g (½ cup) plain (all-purpose) flour
2 eggs, lightly beaten
75g (1 cup) panko breadcrumbs
¼ teaspoon salt
¼ teaspoon ground black pepper
1 teaspoon paprika
4 tablespoons oil
4 brioche rolls, toasted
8 lettuce leaves

Mustard pickle mayo
4 tablespoons mayonnaise
4 tablespoons tomato ketchup
1 tablespoon Dijon mustard
2 tablespoons finely chopped drained pickled gherkins (dill pickles) (I like cocktail gherkins for extra crunch)

1 Make the mustard pickle mayo by placing all the ingredients in a bowl and stirring together. Place in the refrigerator, covered, until ready to use.

2 Now make the fish burgers. Place the fish fillets on pieces of kitchen paper and pat dry.

3 Place the flour in a shallow bowl, the beaten egg in a second bowl and the breadcrumbs in a third bowl. Mix the salt and pepper into the flour. Mix the paprika into the breadcrumbs. Fully coat each piece of fish in the flour, egg and, finally, the breadcrumbs, shaking off any excess as you go.

4 Heat the oil in a frying pan (skillet) over a medium heat until hot. Add the fish burgers to the pan and cook for 4–5 minutes on each side until golden, crisp and cooked all the way through. Remove from the pan and place on a piece of kitchen paper to soak up any excess oil.

5 Place the bottom half of each brioche roll on a plate, top with lettuce, add the fish burger and drizzle on the mustard pickle mayo before topping with the other half of the bun. Serve immediately.

Nicky's pro tips

If you'd prefer to bake the fish, stir 1 tablespoon of oil into the panko breadcrumbs before coating. Place the coated fish fillets on a baking tray and drizzle on another tablespoon of oil. Bake at 190°C fan/410°F/ gas mark 6½ for 10–12 minutes until cooked through and golden.

Champion
Chicken

Chicken. It's the go-to starting point of many dinner recipes. Usually quick to cook (unless you're cooking a whole chicken), it works with so many savoury flavour combinations to tempt even the fussiest of eaters.

I often find myself in front of the refrigerator, asking myself 'What can I make with chicken?' So here is a selection of my favourite quick chicken recipes. Some use ready-cooked chicken – either store-bought rotisserie chicken (a lifesaver when you're making a speedy meal), or leftover cooked chicken. My favourite recipe using ready-cooked chicken is **Tom kha gai** – which is a spicy Thai-style soup that took lots of testing to get it to taste absolutely perfect (see page 80). The kids LOVE **Rotisserie chicken burritos** (see page 83) and **Chicken salsa bake** (see page 79), which suits me down to the ground, as they're easily on the table in 25 minutes.

As for chicken cooked from scratch, my first pick would be the **Crispy chicken with Korean-inspired sauce** (see page 70). It's served up with a big pile of garlicky green beans and it's so good, I could eat it every day!

Naan chicken tikka pizza

A spicy twist on a regular pizza! Juicy marinated chicken tikka pieces are served on top of warm naans, then finished with your favourite toppings. I tend to marinate the chicken in the morning so I can get this on the table quickly for a midweek dinner. If you don't have time beforehand, even a few minutes marinating time will still ensure lovely, tasty chicken.

 Serves 4   Prep time 10 mins   Cook time 15 mins   Total time 25 mins

3 chicken breasts (about 525g/1lb 3oz), chopped into bite-size chunks
120g (½ cup) thick natural yogurt, plus extra to serve
2 garlic cloves, peeled and minced
1 tablespoon minced ginger
1 tablespoon lemon juice (juice of about ½ lemon)
1 teaspoon ground coriander
½ teaspoon ground turmeric
½ teaspoon ground cumin
1 teaspoon paprika
½ teaspoon mild chilli powder
pinch of ground cinnamon
½ teaspoon salt
½ teaspoon ground black pepper
2 tablespoons oil, for brushing onto the chicken before grilling

Naans
4 tablespoons tomato purée (paste)
½ teaspoon sugar
pinch of salt and pepper
3 tablespoons cold water
2 tablespoons finely chopped fresh coriander (cilantro)
• 4 naans (plain or flavoured)

To serve
chilli sauce
finely chopped fresh coriander (cilantro)
flaked almonds

1 Preheat the grill (broiler) to medium–high.

2 Place the chicken in a bowl or freezer bag with the yogurt, garlic, ginger, lemon juice, coriander, turmeric, cumin, paprika, chilli powder, cinnamon, salt and pepper. Mix together so that everything is combined. Marinate if time allows.

3 Spread the chicken out on a grill tray. Brush the chicken with the oil, then place under the grill and cook for 8–10 minutes, turning once.

4 Meanwhile, mix the tomato purée, sugar, salt, pepper, water and coriander in a small bowl.

5 When the chicken is cooked, remove from the grill and put to one side.

6 Place the naans under the grill and cook for 1–2 minutes on each side until hot.

7 Remove the naans and spread the tomato mixture on top, place the breads back under the grill for 1 minute.

8 Remove the naans from the grill and divide the cooked chicken between the breads.

9 Drizzle over the yogurt and chilli sauce. Sprinkle on the coriander and almonds, then serve.

Nicky's pro tips
If you have time, leave the chicken to marinate in the refrigerator for an hour or two (or do it in the morning, ready for dinner later) – this will make the chicken even more flavourful!

Baked gnocchi with chicken & red pesto

££

Store-bought gnocchi are a great staple to have on hand in the refrigerator or freezer to bulk up a meal, while also making it feel a bit 'fancy'. They take big punchy flavours like pesto so well. If you want to change it up, swap out the red pepper pesto for regular basil pesto and you get a totally different meal! There's lots of lovely sauce hidden under the gnocchi in this recipe, so I recommend serving with crusty bread for dunking.

 Serves 4   Prep time 5 mins   Cook time 25 mins   Total time 30 mins

2 chicken breasts (350g/12oz), chopped into bite-size pieces
1 tablespoon olive oil
¼ teaspoon salt
¼ teaspoon ground black pepper, plus extra to serve
½ teaspoon dried oregano
60g (2 packed cups) baby spinach
120ml (½ cup) hot chicken stock
500g (1lb 2oz) pack fresh gnocchi (if using frozen, defrost it)
8 tablespoons (140g/5oz) Red pepper pesto (see page 196)
1 red (bell) pepper, deseeded and sliced
60ml (¼ cup) double (heavy) cream
1 tablespoon tomato purée (paste)
150g (5½oz) mozzarella ball, torn into small pieces

To serve
a handful fresh basil leaves
chunks of crusty bread, for dunking

1 Preheat the oven to 200°C fan/425°F/gas mark 7.

2 Place the chicken pieces in a medium baking dish. Drizzle over the oil and sprinkle on the salt, pepper and oregano. Toss together to coat the chicken evenly.

3 Bake in the oven for 10 minutes.

4 Remove the dish from the oven and add the spinach, then pour over the hot stock. Add the gnocchi, pesto, red pepper, cream and tomato purée. Stir everything together to combine. Dot the torn mozzarella among the chicken and gnocchi pieces.

5 Return to the oven for a further 15 minutes until the chicken is cooked through and the sauce is bubbling.

6 Serve topped with basil leaves and a sprinkling of black pepper, alongside some crusty bread.

Make it vegetarian

Swap the chicken for chunky pieces of courgette (zucchini). Swap the chicken stock for vegetable stock. Ensure you're using vegetarian mozzarella and pesto.

Champion Chicken

Chicken & chilli sauce traybake

This is a simple hands-off method of getting a dinner on the table quickly.
Everything is added to the tray at the start, then it all cooks together in the oven.
The addition of cornflour helps the sauce to thicken as it cooks.

 Serves 4   **Prep time** 5 mins   **Cook time** 20–25 mins   **Total time** 25–30 mins

3 chicken breasts (about 525g/1lb 3oz), chopped into bite-size pieces

1 onion, peeled and chopped into thin wedges

1 red (bell) pepper, deseeded and sliced

Sauce

2 garlic cloves, peeled and minced

1 teaspoon minced ginger

½ teaspoon salt

½ teaspoon ground black pepper

1½ tablespoons cornflour (cornstarch)

2 tablespoons Chinese rice wine

4 tablespoons light brown sugar

2 teaspoons chilli (red pepper) flakes

2 tablespoons tomato ketchup

1 tablespoon oil

240ml (1 cup) hot chicken stock

To serve

chopped spring onions (scallions)

sesame seeds

chilli (red pepper) flakes

cooked rice or noodles

1 Preheat the oven to 220°C fan/475°F/gas mark 9.

2 Place the chicken, onion and red pepper into a shallow roasting tray.

3 Mix together all of the sauce ingredients, except for the chicken stock Once incorporated, stir the chicken stock into the sauce and pour all over the chicken and vegetables.

4 Cook in the oven for 20–25 minutes, stirring once halfway through cooking, until the chicken is cooked through and golden brown. You can check this by slicing into a piece of chicken and ensuring it's piping hot and no longer pink in the middle.

5 Serve topped with spring onions, sesame seeds and chilli flakes. I love to serve this with boiled rice or noodles.

Nicky's pro tips

You can add more vegetables, such as green beans, broccoli or sugar snap peas (snow peas) to this dish. Add them for the last 15 minutes of cooking. If you add more vegetables, it will take a little longer to cook. Just ensure your vegetables are tender and the chicken is piping hot throughout and no longer pink in the middle before serving.

Crispy chicken with Korean-inspired sauce & garlic green beans

I like to flatten/tenderize the chicken in this recipe for a quick cooking time. My family loves the resultant 'giant chicken steaks', which work so well with the spicy-sweet gochujang sauce. You can serve it up with rice, crispy potatoes or salad, but my favourite side dish for this recipe is a giant pile of garlicky green beans!

 Serves 4   **Prep time** 10 mins   **Cook time** 20 mins   **Total time** 30 mins

4 chicken breasts

2 eggs, lightly beaten

4 tablespoons plain (all-purpose) flour

¼ teaspoon salt

¼ teaspoon ground black pepper

75g (1½ cups) panko breadcrumbs

½ teaspoon paprika

6 tablespoons oil, for frying

Korean-inspired sauce

1 tablespoon gochujang paste

2 tablespoons honey

4 tablespoons light brown sugar

2 tablespoons dark soy sauce

1 garlic clove, peeled and minced

1 tablespoon cornflour (cornstarch)

180ml (¾ cup) chicken stock

Garlic green beans

450g (1lb) fresh green beans, ends trimmed

½ tablespoon olive oil

½ tablespoon unsalted butter

2 garlic cloves, peeled and minced

¼ teaspoon salt

¼ teaspoon ground black pepper

1 teaspoon lemon juice

1 Place a baking tray in the oven and preheat the oven to a low heat (about 90°C fan/200°F/gas mark ½), to keep the chicken warm, once cooked.

2 Place the chicken breasts between pieces of clingfilm (plastic wrap) and bash with a meat tenderizer or rolling pin to flatten, so the chicken breasts are half as thick.

3 Place the eggs in a shallow bowl, the flour, salt and pepper in a second bowl (mixed together) and the panko breadcrumbs and paprika in a third bowl.

4 Coat one of the chicken steaks in the flour, then dip in the egg and finally coat in the breadcrumbs. Place on a plate and repeat with the other chicken steaks.

5 Working in two batches, heat 3 tablespoons of the oil in a large frying pan (skillet) and fry two of the chicken steaks over a medium heat for 5 minutes on each side until golden brown and cooked throughout (you can check this by slicing into one of the chicken steaks and making sure it's piping hot and no longer pink). Place the first batch on the tray in the preheated oven to keep warm. Add the remaining 3 tablespoons of oil to the pan and cook the remaining two chicken steaks.

6 While the chicken is cooking, make the Korean-inspired sauce and garlic green beans. Place the gochujang, honey, sugar, soy sauce, garlic and cornflour in a small saucepan and stir together until the cornflour is absorbed.

7 Add the chicken stock and stir again. Place over a medium heat and heat through for 5 minutes, stirring occasionally, then reduce the heat to very low to keep warm while you make the green beans.

8 Put the green beans in a large pan of boiling water, cook for 3 minutes then drain and refresh under cold running water – that is what helps keep their vibrant colour.

9 Heat the oil and butter in a large frying pan (skillet) over a medium heat until the butter melts, then add the green beans, garlic, salt and pepper. Cook the green beans, stirring often, for 3–4 minutes until just tender. Then drizzle over the lemon juice. Turn off the heat.

10 Serve the crispy chicken steaks with the garlic green beans. Drizzle with the Korean-inspired sauce before serving.

Nicky's pro tips

This recipe requires a bit of multi-tasking – making the sauce and green beans while frying the chicken. If you want to make it simpler, cook the chicken first, then keep warm in a low oven. Then you can make the sauce, followed by the green beans.

Champion Chicken

Chicken pot pie soup with puff pastry squares

££

A light and creamy soup made using ready-cooked chicken and frozen vegetables. It becomes a 'proper meal' with the addition of pastry squares to make it more filling. Everyone gets a pastry square on their soup, then two on the side for extra pastry satisfaction!

 Serves 4

 Prep time 10 mins

Cook time 15 mins

 Total time 25 mins

3 tablespoons unsalted butter
3 tablespoons plain (all-purpose) flour
600ml (2½ cups) chicken stock (water plus 3 stock/bouillon cubes is fine)
300ml (1¼ cups) full-fat (whole) milk
1 tablespoon lemon juice (juice of about ½ lemon)
400g (14oz) frozen vegetable mix
¼ teaspoon salt
¼ teaspoon ground black pepper
a pinch of dried thyme
2 cooked chicken breasts (about 150g/5½oz each), shredded

Pastry
1 x 320g (11½oz) packet of ready-rolled puff pastry
1 small egg, lightly beaten
¼ teaspoon dried thyme

1   Preheat the oven to 200°C fan/425°F/gas mark 7 and line a baking sheet with non-stick parchment or a non-stick baking mat.

2   Unroll the pastry, brush on the egg wash and sprinkle over the dried thyme.

3   Cut the pastry into 12 equal squares and place on the prepared baking sheet. Bake in the oven for 15 minutes until puffed up and golden brown. Remove from the oven.

4   Meanwhile, melt the butter in a large saucepan over a medium heat. Add the flour and stir constantly, using a whisk, for 1 minute until the flour is fully incorporated and the flour mixture is bubbling slightly.

5   Slowly pour in the chicken stock, while stirring with the whisk constantly. At first it will form a thick paste, but as you add more stock, it will thin out.

6   Add the milk, turn up the heat to medium–high and continue to stir constantly. As the liquid comes to the boil, it should thicken.

7   Once it comes to the boil, add the lemon juice, frozen vegetables, salt, pepper and thyme. Give it a stir and simmer for 5 minutes until the vegetables are tender.

8   Add the shredded cooked chicken, stir and cook for a further 3–4 minutes until the chicken is heated through.

9   Turn off the heat and spoon the soup into bowls. Top each bowl with a pastry square. Serve with the remaining pastry squares.

Nicky's pro tips
I sometimes like to add potatoes into this soup. Simply peel and dice 2 medium potatoes, then simmer with the stock and milk for 10 minutes before adding the frozen vegetables.

Sticky chicken thighs with chilli & lime

££

Juicy, tender chicken thighs, pan-fried until golden brown and then simmered with a sticky, zingy and slightly spicy, chilli and lime sauce. Served on top of fluffy boiled rice, this is a lovely quick dinner.

Serves 4   **Prep time** 5 mins   **Cook time** 12 mins   **Total time** 17 mins

8 chicken thigh fillets, trimmed of excess fat and flattened out with your hands
3 tablespoons cornflour (cornstarch)
½ teaspoon salt
½ teaspoon ground black pepper
1 tablespoon sesame oil
1 tablespoon rapeseed (canola) oil
2 tablespoons light soy sauce
4 tablespoons lime juice (juice of about 2 limes)
2 tablespoons honey
2 tablespoons light brown sugar
3 garlic cloves, peeled and minced
2 red chillies, sliced

To serve
sesame seeds
chilli (red pepper) flakes
lime wedges
sliced spring onions (scallions)
boiled rice or noodles

1   Place the chicken thigh fillets on a plate. Mix together 2 tablespoons of the cornflour with the salt and pepper and sprinkle it on both sides of the chicken thighs.

2   Heat the sesame and rapeseed oils in a large frying pan (skillet) over a medium–high heat. Add the chicken thighs and fry for 6–7 minutes, turning once, until golden.

3   Meanwhile, mix together the soy sauce, lime juice, honey, sugar, garlic, chillies and remaining tablespoon of cornflour in a small bowl.

4   Once the chicken is golden brown, pour the mixture all over the chicken thighs, in the pan. Bring to the boil, then simmer for 5 minutes until the sauce has thickened.

5   Top the chicken with sesame seeds, chilli flakes, lime slices and sliced spring onions, then serve. I love these with boiled rice or noodles.

Nicky's pro tips

Replace the 8 chicken thighs with 4 chicken breasts if you prefer. Place the chicken breasts between pieces of clingfilm (plastic wrap) and bash with a meat tenderizer or rolling pin to flatten, so the chicken breasts are half as thick. This will help them cook more quickly and evenly.

Champion Chicken

75

Chicken in creamy honey mustard sauce

££

This sauce is lip-smackingly delicious. If you like a bit of heat, you can replace the Dijon mustard with hot English mustard (start with a little, then taste as you add more for the perfect heat level). You can also use wholegrain mustard for a different texture, but with the same mild heat level as Dijon.

 Serves
4

 Prep time
10 mins

 Cook time
15 mins

 Total time
25 mins

2 large chicken breasts (about 200g/7oz each), sliced in half horizontally to make 4 fillets
1 teaspoon salt
1 teaspoon ground black pepper, plus extra to serve
1 teaspoon paprika
1 teaspoon dried thyme
1 tablespoon oil
1 tablespoon unsalted butter
1 onion, peeled and finely chopped
3 garlic cloves, peeled and minced
120ml (½ cup) chicken stock
2 tablespoons Dijon mustard
2 tablespoons honey
120ml (½ cup) double (heavy) cream

To serve
chopped fresh flat-leaf parsley
green vegetables, such as green beans or peas
baby new potatoes or boiled rice

1. Place the chicken fillets on a plate. Mix together the salt, pepper, paprika and thyme and sprinkle all over the chicken on both sides.

2. Heat the oil and butter in a large frying pan (skillet) over a medium–high heat until the butter starts to foam. Add the chicken fillets to the pan and cook for 3 minutes on each side until lightly golden.

3. Move the fillets over to one side of the pan (it's fine to pile them on top of each other) and add the onion and garlic to the space in the pan. Cook for 3–4 minutes, stirring, until the onion softens. Move the chicken around a little too, so it continues to cook evenly.

4. Add the chicken stock, mustard and honey to the pan and stir together, so the mustard is incorporated into the sauce.

5. Add the cream and stir, then arrange the chicken fillets evenly in the pan. Simmer for 4–5 minutes until the chicken is completely cooked through (you can check this by slicing the thickest part of one of the chicken fillets open, it should be piping hot and no longer pink in the middle).

6. Serve the chicken sprinkled with parsley and black pepper. I like to serve mine with green vegetables and baby new potatoes or rice.

Nicky's pro tips

If you're serving this with potatoes or rice, put them on to cook just before you start preparing the chicken, so they're ready at the same time as the chicken. Green beans or peas can be steamed/boiled for 5–8 minutes or you could add them to the pan with the chicken and sauce at the same time you add the stock, then simmer everything together until the chicken is cooked and the vegetables are tender.

Chicken salsa bake

Salsa isn't just for dipping! It can be used as a simple ready-seasoned sauce (which is why I don't use salt and pepper in this recipe). The kids go wild for this dish as a weekend treat – all served up in big scoops alongside a mountain of nachos!

Serves 4   **Prep time** 15 mins   **Cook time** 15 mins   **Total time** 30 mins

1 cooked rotisserie chicken

1 red (bell) pepper, deseeded and chopped into small chunks (about 1cm/½in)

2 tablespoons pickled jalapeños, drained, plus extra to serve

1 small onion, peeled and thinly sliced

1 tablespoon oil

1 tablespoon tomato purée (paste)

2 tablespoons fajita seasoning (you can buy this ready-made from the supermarket)

300g (10½oz) jar of chunky salsa (mild or hot, depending on your preference)

100g (1 packed cup) grated (shredded) mixed cheese (I use a mixture of Cheddar, firm mozzarella and red Leicester)

To serve

½ red onion, peeled and finely diced

fresh coriander (cilantro), roughly chopped

tortilla crisps

1. Preheat the oven to 200°C fan/425°F/gas mark 7.

2. Remove all the meat from the rotisserie chicken and shred, then place in a shallow roasting tray. Add the red pepper, jalapeños, onion, oil, tomato purée and fajita seasoning. Toss together to coat everything in the fajita seasoning.

3. Pour over the salsa, then sprinkle on the cheese. Bake in the oven for 15 minutes until the cheese is melted and bubbling.

4. Remove from the oven and sprinkle on the red onion, coriander and more jalapeños. Serve with tortilla crisps.

Nicky's pro tips

For a put-in-the-middle-of-the-table-and-dig-in dish, warm the nachos on a tray in the oven for 5 minutes, then arrange on a large serving plate. Carefully spoon the cooked cheesy chicken salsa on top (I slide it out of the dish with the help of a spatula, so the melted cheese stays on top), sprinkle on the onion, coriander and jalapeños and serve with sour cream.

Champion Chicken

Tom kha gai

This soup is my FAVOURITE thing to order from our local Thai takeaway.
A spicy soup, made with coconut milk, galangal, lemongrass, shiitake
mushrooms, chillies and chicken. I'm not kidding, it will blow your mind!
It makes a fantastic lunch or starter, or you can serve it with a bowl of boiled rice
for dinner. Take a spoonful of rice and dunk it in the soup. Bliss!

 Serves 4   **Prep time** 10 mins   **Cook time** 15 mins   **Total time** 25 mins

1 tablespoon oil

1 onion, peeled and finely chopped

3 garlic cloves, peeled and minced

2 teaspoons galangal paste, or a 2cm (¾in) piece of galangal, peeled and finely chopped

1 lemongrass stalk, tough outer leaves removed and inner stalk sliced finely (or 1 teaspoon lemongrass paste)

4 makrut lime leaves

2 red chillies, sliced (Fresno but you can use Thai chillies if you like the extra heat)

10 shiitake mushrooms, sliced in half

1 heaped tablespoon red Thai curry paste

1 litre (4¼ cups) chicken stock

1 x 400ml (14fl oz) can full-fat coconut milk

1 tablespoon fish sauce

1 tablespoon light brown sugar

juice of 1 lime (about 2 tablespoons)

6 cooked chicken thigh fillets, shredded

1 tablespoon cornflour (cornstarch), mixed with 3 tablespoons cold water to form a slurry (optional)

To serve

a small bunch of fresh coriander (cilantro), roughly torn

2 teaspoons chilli oil

1 lime, sliced

1   Heat the oil in a large saucepan over a medium heat. Add the onion and cook for 5 minutes, stirring often, until softened.

2   Add the garlic, galangal paste, lemongrass, lime leaves, chillies, mushrooms and Thai curry paste. Cook for 1 minute, stirring often.

3   Add the chicken stock, coconut milk, fish sauce, sugar, lime juice and shredded chicken. Bring to the boil and simmer for 5–6 minutes until the chicken is fully heated through. If you would like to thicken the soup at all, slowly pour in the cornflour slurry, stirring.

4   Taste the soup and season with a little salt and pepper if needed.

5   Divide between bowls, then top with fresh coriander and drizzle with a little chilli oil. Top with slices of lime before serving.

> 💬 *Nicky's pro tips*
>
> Make the soup ahead, then cool, cover and refrigerate. Reheat in a pan over a medium heat, stirring occasionally, until piping hot.
>
> 🍖 *Make it vegetarian*
>
> Leave out the chicken or swap it for a vegetarian chicken alternative. Leave out the fish sauce and swap the chicken stock for good-quality vegetable stock. I would also add some extra mushrooms.

Make it vegetarian

Swap the chicken for your favourite vegetarian alternative. Fried mushrooms, halloumi and vegetarian chicken-style pieces work well.

Rotisserie chicken burritos

We're using all the shortcuts to get these burritos on the table quickly. Ready-cooked rotisserie chicken, microwave rice and canned beans in chilli sauce are great speedy ingredients that only need warming through. I like to spice things up by adding fajita seasoning to the chicken and some pickled jalapeños at the end too. Grate (shred) the cheese finely, then it will melt into the chicken and rice once it's all rolled up.

 Serves 4   **Prep time** 15 mins   **Cook time** 15 mins   **Total time** 30 mins

4 large flour tortillas, warmed in the oven or microwave
1 small cooked rotisserie chicken
2 tablespoons oil
1 small onion, peeled and diced
2 tablespoons fajita seasoning
¼ teaspoon salt
¼ teaspoon ground black pepper
1 x 400g (14oz) can mixed beans in chilli sauce (or use Mexican refried beans)
1 x 250g (9oz) pack ready-cooked rice (plain or flavoured – Mexican style is a good choice)
75g (¾ cup) finely grated (shredded) Cheddar
2 tablespoons pickled jalapeños, drained and roughly chopped
a small bunch of fresh coriander (cilantro), roughly chopped
4 tablespoons tomato salsa
4 tablespoons sour cream
1 little gem lettuce, washed and torn into individual leaves

1. Place the cooked chicken on a board and slice or tear off the meat. Break into bite-size shreds.

2. Heat the oil in a large frying pan (skillet) over a medium–high heat. Add the onion, chicken, fajita seasoning, salt and pepper. Toss together and fry for 5–6 minutes, stirring often, until the chicken is hot and the onion starts to soften.

3. Move the chicken to the side of the pan. Add the beans in chilli sauce and heat through for 5–6 minutes, stirring often and squishing the beans with the back of a spoon as they heat through. Stir the chicken a few times too, so it doesn't burn.

4. While the chicken and beans are cooking, heat the rice, as per the packet instructions (usually a couple of minutes in the microwave).

5. Lay out four large pieces of foil and place a warmed tortilla on each piece of foil.

6. Divide the rice, chicken and beans between the tortillas. Try to arrange on the bottom half of each tortilla (so it's easier to roll up later). Top with the cheese, jalapeños, coriander, salsa and sour cream, then layer a couple of lettuce leaves on top.

7. Roll the burrito up, tucking the ends in as you roll. Wrap in the foil and twist the ends, then serve.

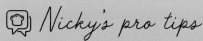 Nicky's pro tips

You can make these ahead of time, but if you do, leave out the lettuce and sour cream (they're not great reheated – use the sour cream as a dip instead). Make up and wrap the burritos in foil, then cool and refrigerate for up to a day. Reheat in the oven (in the foil) for 15–20 minutes at 180°C fan/400°F/gas mark 6 until piping hot throughout.

Black pepper chicken

Although black pepper beef is more well-known, this dish also works really well with chicken (and is a little more economical too). The black pepper in this stir-fry provides a lovely warmth, rather than the sometimes fiery heat of chillies.

 Serves 4   **Prep time** 10 mins   **Cook time** 12 mins   **Total time** 22 mins

3 chicken breasts (about 525g/1lb 3oz), sliced into thin strips

¼ teaspoon salt

2 teaspoons ground black pepper

2 tablespoons rapeseed (canola) oil

1 teaspoon sesame oil

1 large onion, peeled and thickly sliced

1 green (bell) pepper, deseeded and sliced

1 red (bell) pepper, deseeded and sliced

2 garlic cloves, peeled and minced

1 teaspoon minced ginger

2 tablespoons cornflour (cornstarch)

2 tablespoons dark soy sauce

2 tablespoons oyster sauce

1 tablespoon Chinese rice wine or dry sherry

120ml (½ cup) chicken stock

To serve

boiled rice

spring onions (scallions), chopped

1   Toss the chicken strips with the salt and 1 teaspoon of the black pepper.

2   Heat the rapeseed and sesame oils in a wok (or large frying pan/skillet) over a high heat until hot, then add the chicken. Stir-fry the chicken for 5 minutes, moving it around the wok so it doesn't stick together, until lightly browned.

3   Reduce the heat to medium–high. Add the onion, peppers, garlic and ginger. Stir-fry for 3–4 minutes, frequently tossing everything together with a spatula, until the vegetables are just starting to soften.

4   While the chicken and vegetables are cooking, add the cornflour, dark soy sauce, oyster sauce and Chinese rice wine to a small jug or bowl and stir together until the cornflour is incorporated. Add the chicken stock and the remaining teaspoon of black pepper. Stir together to combine.

5   Add the sauce to the wok and stir together. Heat for 1–2 minutes, allowing it to come to a gentle simmer. If it looks too thick, add in a splash of water. Turn off the heat.

6   Serve the black pepper chicken with boiled rice and a sprinkling of chopped spring onions.

🗨️ *Nicky's pro tips*

This dish reheats well (although the peppers will be softer), so if you want to get ahead you can make it, then quickly cool, cover and refrigerate for up to a day. Remove from the refrigerator 30 minutes before reheating to take the chill off it, then reheat in a wok over a medium–high heat for 5–6 minutes until piping hot throughout. Stir often to prevent it sticking and add in a good splash of water or stock to help loosen the sauce.

Honey lemon chicken

£££

Succulent chicken breasts are cooked in a fresh and zesty sauce with just the right amount of honey sweetness. This dish works equally well with rice or pasta. If you make enough for leftovers, it also tastes amazing sliced up and tossed with salad leaves for lunch.

 Serves 4   **Prep time** 5 mins   **Cook time** 15 mins   **Total time** 20 mins

2 large chicken breasts (about 200g/7oz each), sliced in half horizontally, to make 4 fillets
3 tablespoons plain (all-purpose) flour
½ teaspoon salt
½ teaspoon ground black pepper
½ teaspoon paprika
1 tablespoon olive oil
2 tablespoons unsalted butter
2 garlic cloves, peeled and minced
120ml (½ cup) chicken stock
4 tablespoons fresh lemon juice (juice from about 1½–2 lemons)
3 tablespoons honey
1 lemon, sliced into half-moons

To serve

1 tablespoon chopped fresh flat-leaf parsley
boiled rice, spaghetti, linguine or orzo

1 Place the chicken fillets on a plate or a metal tray. Mix together the flour, salt, pepper and paprika. Coat both sides of the chicken with the flour mixture.

2 Heat the oil and butter in a large frying pan (skillet) over a medium–high heat until the butter melts.

3 Add the fillets to the pan and cook for 7–8 minutes, turning once, until both sides are golden brown.

4 Add the garlic, stir for 30 seconds (don't let the garlic burn), then add the chicken stock, lemon juice, honey and lemon slices. Bring to the boil and simmer for 5 minutes until the sauce is slightly reduced (simmer for a few minutes longer if you want the sauce a little thicker).

5 Sprinkle with fresh parsley and serve with rice or pasta.

Nicky's pro tips

Add some heat with 1 tablespoon of sweet chilli sauce or 1 teaspoon of sriracha to the sauce.

Champion Chicken

Chicken fried rice

I love this quick recipe for takeaway-style chicken fried rice. It's a great way to use up leftover scraps of chicken from your roast dinner and it's easy to change up with whatever you have on hand to make it a little different each time.

 Serves 4   Prep time 10 mins   Cook time 15 mins   Total time 25 mins

2 tablespoons rapeseed (canola) oil
1 onion, peeled and diced
1 red (bell) pepper, deseeded and finely chopped
2 garlic cloves, peeled and minced
115g (⅔ cup) frozen peas
250g (2 cups) shredded or sliced cooked chicken (light or dark meat)
½ tablespoon sesame oil
800g (4 cups) boiled and cooled long-grain rice (about 300g/⅓ cups dried rice)
2 eggs
2 tablespoons dark soy sauce
¼ teaspoon salt
1 tablespoon lemon juice (juice of about ½ lemon)
4 spring onions (scallions), chopped, to serve

1 Heat 1 tablespoon of the rapeseed oil in a large wok over a medium heat. Add the onion and cook, stirring regularly, for 5 minutes until it starts to turn soft and translucent.

2 Add the remaining rapeseed oil, the red pepper, garlic and peas. Cook for a further 2 minutes, stirring regularly.

3 Now add the chicken and sesame oil. Stir together, then add the rice and turn the heat up to high. Use a spatula to toss everything together and to ensure the rice doesn't stick to the bottom of the wok. Keep moving the rice around so it heats up evenly.

4 Once the rice is hot (this will take about 5 minutes), push the rice over to the side of the wok and crack the eggs into the space. Add a little splash of the soy sauce to the eggs.

5 Making sure the part of the wok with the eggs in is over the heat, fry the eggs, giving a mix with the spatula until the egg starts to cook and look scrambled, but is still a little runny. Now mix the egg into the rice.

6 Pour in the remaining soy sauce and sprinkle on the salt and mix it all together.

7 Add the lemon juice, stir and taste. Add a little more lemon juice if required.

8 Serve topped with the spring onions.

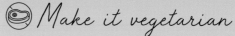 *Nicky's pro tips*

Always use cold boiled rice (ideally boil the rice the day before, then cool, cover and chill it to use the next day). This stops your fried rice from being soggy or sticky and ensures the rice absorbs more flavour too.

Make it vegetarian

Swap out the chicken for strips/shreds of your favourite meat replacement. Vegetarian shredded duck or chicken alternatives work well.

Moreish
Meat

This chapter was my favourite section of this book to write (and test!). Initially I was worried, as a lot of (non-chicken) meat-based dishes can take longer than 30 minutes to put together. But with some specific cuts of meat, a few flavour hacks and my husband's dedication to repeatedly taste-testing meaty recipes (such a trooper), we got there and I'm so excited about every single one of these recipes.

The **Steaky chips with peppercorn sauce** (see page 108) – which was inspired by a dish they sell at a local beach restaurant in my town – has been made on repeat nearly every week since I first tested the recipe!

I urge you to try the **Minute steak curry** (see page 107) – yes, a quick curry can be made with beef and still be tender and delicious.

As for the **Potato & bacon hash with cheesy beans** (see page 99), well that's just pure comfort food in a bowl. Possibly it's a bit more on the breakfast side of things, but I'm all for breakfast for dinner!

Gnocchi with chorizo & creamy harissa

££

Here's a bit of a different way to pep-up store-bought gnocchi and turn them into something really special. I love the spicy-smokiness of harissa paste, which is made from a blend of chillies, spices and herbs. If you've never used it before, go with rose harissa, which is a little milder than regular harissa.

 Serves 4

 Prep time 10 mins

 Cook time 20 mins

Total time 30 mins

1 teaspoon oil
150g (5½oz) chorizo, diced (I favour the ready-chopped)
1 small onion, peeled and finely diced
1 red (bell) pepper, deseeded and sliced
2 garlic cloves, peeled and minced
¼ teaspoon salt
¼ teaspoons ground black pepper
1½ tablespoon harissa paste
1 tablespoon tomato purée (paste)
200ml (¾ cup + 1 tablespoon) full-fat coconut milk
150g (5½oz) cherry tomatoes, sliced in half
500g (1lb 2oz) fresh gnocchi
60g (2 packed cups) baby spinach

To serve
chilli (red pepper) flakes
ground black pepper
chopped fresh flat-leaf parsley

1 Heat the oil in a large frying pan (skillet) over a medium–high heat. Add the chorizo and cook, stirring often, for 3–4 minutes until it starts to release its oils. Use a slotted spoon to remove the chorizo to a bowl and set aside.

2 Reduce the heat to medium and add the onion, red pepper, garlic, salt and pepper. Cook for 5 minutes, stirring often, until the onion and pepper soften.

3 Meanwhile, bring a large pan of water to the boil for the gnocchi.

4 Add the harissa paste and tomato purée to the pan with the onion and stir together. Add the coconut milk and cherry tomatoes, stir and bring to a simmer. Simmer for 5 minutes, stirring occasionally.

5 Meanwhile, add the gnocchi to the pan of boiling water and cook for 2–4 minutes until they float to the top of the pan.

6 Once the gnocchi are cooked, use a slotted spoon to remove them from the water and place directly in the pan with the sauce.

7 Add the spinach and the cooked chorizo. Stir together and cook for a further 1–2 minutes until the spinach wilts.

8 Serve topped with chilli flakes, black pepper and parsley.

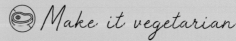 *Nicky's pro tips*
Swap out the chorizo for crispy bacon, or you could even add in chunks of cooked chicken, pork or prawns (shrimp).

Make it vegetarian
Swap out the chorizo for a vegetarian-style chorizo or salami slices.

Pork chops in creamy mustard sauce

££

These succulent pork chops are pan-fried and finished in the oven, all served with a warming, creamy mustard sauce. The sauce is made while the pork is in the oven, so it's all ready at the same time.

 Serves 4   Prep time 5 mins   Cook time 25 mins   Total time 30 mins

4 thick-cut, bone-in, pork chops
½ teaspoon salt
½ teaspoon ground black pepper
1½ tablespoons oil
240 ml (1 cup) chicken stock
1 heaped tablespoon wholegrain mustard
120ml (½ cup) double (heavy) cream
1 dash (about ⅛ teaspoon) Worcestershire sauce

To serve
2 tablespoons chopped fresh flat-leaf parsley
ground black pepper
steamed baby potatoes
steamed green beans

1   Preheat the oven to 175°C fan/375°F/gas mark 5.

2   Place the pork chops on a plate and sprinkle on the salt and pepper.

3   Heat the oil in a large pan over a high heat. Place the pork chops in the pan and cook for about 3 minutes on each side until browned.

4   Transfer the pork to a baking tray and cook in the oven for 5–6 minutes until the pork is no longer pink in the middle.

5   Meanwhile, reduce the heat under the pan to medium and add the chicken stock to the pan. Heat for 3–4 minutes, giving the stock a stir, to deglaze the pan.

6   Stir in the mustard, then stir the cream and Worcestershire sauce. Bring to the boil, then simmer gently for 5 minutes until the sauce thickens slightly.

7   When the pork is ready, remove from the oven and place on a warm plate to rest for 3–4 minutes.

8   Divide the rested pork between plates and pour over the sauce. Sprinkle with parsley and black pepper and serve. I love to serve mine with steamed baby potatoes and green beans.

💬 *Nicky's pro tips*
Use crème fraîche instead of double (heavy) cream for a lighter sauce.

Moreish Meat

Stir-fried pork in pineapple chilli sauce

A sweet-spicy stir-fry that uses canned pineapple, both fruit and juice, as the base of this simple sauce. If you're cooking it for kids, you can leave the sriracha and chilli out entirely and it still works well with more of a sweet and sour flavour.

 Serves 4   **Prep time** 15 mins   **Cook time** 10 mins   **Total time** 25 mins

2 tablespoons oil
500g (1lb 2oz) pork tenderloin, sliced into thin strips, against the grain
¼ teaspoon salt
¼ teaspoon ground black pepper
2 garlic cloves, peeled and minced
2 teaspoons ginger paste
200g (1⅓ cups) mangetout
1 red (bell) pepper, deseeded and sliced
1 red chilli, sliced
1 x 430g (15oz) can pineapple chunks in juice

Pineapple chilli sauce
juice from 1 x 430g (15oz) can pineapple chunks (or 120ml/½ cup pineapple juice)
1 tablespoon white wine vinegar
2 tablespoons caster (superfine) sugar
2 tablespoons tomato purée (paste)
2 tablespoons light soy sauce
1–2 tablespoons sriracha (depending on how hot you like it)
1 tablespoon cornflour (cornstarch)
180ml (¾ cup) chicken stock

To serve
boiled rice or noodles
chopped spring onions (scallions)
chilli (red pepper) flakes

1. First, make the pineapple chilli sauce by mixing together the pineapple juice, vinegar, sugar, tomato purée, soy sauce, sriracha and cornflour in a bowl or jug until the cornflour is fully combined. Then add the chicken stock and stir again. Set aside.

2. Heat the oil in a wok over a high heat.

3. Toss the pork in the salt and pepper and add to the wok. Cook for 3–4 minutes, frequently moving everything around the wok with a spatula, until the pork is lightly browned.

4. Add the garlic, ginger, mangetout, red pepper, chilli and pineapple chunks and fry for 3 minutes, tossing everything around in the wok constantly, until the vegetables and pineapple are hot (we want them to retain their crunch, though).

5. Add the sauce and cook for a further 2–3 minutes, stirring often, until hot.

6. Serve with boiled rice or noodles, topped with spring onions and chilli flakes.

Nicky's pro tips

I use pork tenderloin, which is great for a quick stir-fry as it's a tender cut of meat. However, if you wanted to use other cuts – such as shoulder or leg, you can 'velvet' them first – to make them softer and more tender. Cut the pork into thin slices or bite-size cubes and place in a bowl with 240ml (1 cup) of cold water plus 2 teaspoons of bicarbonate of soda (baking soda). Stir and allow to sit for 30 minutes (up to 2 hours), then rinse off and pat dry with kitchen paper. Use as per the recipe above.

Potato & bacon hash with cheesy beans

£

This is a bit of a breakfast-for-dinner type meal. A simple seasoned potato hash with crispy bacon, served alongside good ol' baked beans that have been given a big flavour boost with smoky paprika, warming white pepper and creamy cheese. I love this for a comforting dinner, or a relaxed weekend brunch.

 Serves 4

 Prep time 10 mins

 Cook time 20 mins

 Total time 30 mins

500g (1lb 2oz) potatoes, peeled and chopped into 1.5cm (⅝in) cubes
2 tablespoons oil
8 rashers (strips) streaky bacon
1 small onion, peeled and chopped into small chunks
¼ teaspoon salt
¼ teaspoon ground black pepper
¼ teaspoon garlic powder

Cheesy beans
2 x 400g (14oz) cans baked beans
1 teaspoon smoked paprika
⅛ teaspoon white pepper
100g (1 packed cup) grated (shredded) mixed cheese (I use red Leicester, Cheddar and mozzarella, bought ready-grated/pre-shredded)

To serve
a good pinch of ground black pepper
2 spring onions (scallions), finely chopped

1 Place the potatoes in a pan and cover with cold water. Set over a high heat. Bring to the boil, then reduce the heat and simmer for 5 minutes.

2 Meanwhile, heat ½ tablespoon of the oil in a large frying pan (skillet) over a medium–high heat. Add the bacon and fry for 5 minutes, turning once, until crisp. Remove from the pan and place on a chopping board.

3 When the potatoes are par-boiled, turn off the heat and drain them.

4 Add the remaining oil to the frying pan you used to cook the bacon. Heat over a medium heat.

5 Add the drained potatoes to the pan in a single layer and cook for 4–5 minutes. Try not to move them around too much, so they brown nicely, but keep an eye on them to ensure they don't burn.

6 While the potatoes are cooking, add the beans, paprika and white pepper to a saucepan over a medium heat and stir occasionally until hot. Then reduce the heat to very low, to keep the beans warm.

7 Use a spatula to turn the potatoes over in the pan. Add the onion, salt, black pepper and garlic powder. Cook the potatoes, turning occasionally, for a further 5 minutes until the onion softens.

8 Chop the bacon into small pieces and add to the pan with the potatoes. Stir together and cook for a further 1–2 minutes to heat the bacon through. Then turn off the heat.

9 Add half of the cheese mix to the beans. Stir together, then turn off the heat.

10 Divide the potato mixture between plates and spoon the beans on the side. Sprinkle the remaining cheese on top of the beans. Finish the dish with a sprinkling of black pepper and spring onions, then serve.

🍳 Nicky's pro tips
This recipe also works well with canned potatoes. Simply drain, slice in half and add to the frying pan (no-need to par-boil).

Moreish Meat

Pork & lemongrass meatballs with noodles

£££

Lemongrass adds a delicious fragrance and slightly citrusy flavour to these spicy meatballs. They're served in a warming savoury sauce with a hint of sweet and sour flavour that makes it totally scrumptious. Serve with fresh egg noodles (usually in the salad section of the supermarket), which can be quickly heated up in the sauce.

 Serves 4   **Prep time** 15 mins   **Cook time** 15 mins   **Total time** 30 mins

2 tablespoons oil

500g (1lb 2oz) fresh (cooked) egg noodles

15g (about ¼ packed cup) finely chopped fresh coriander (cilantro) leaves

1 teaspoon black sesame seeds, to serve

Sauce

2 tablespoons light soy sauce

2 tablespoons lime juice (about juice of 1 lime)

2 tablespoons light brown sugar

2 garlic cloves, peeled and minced

1 teaspoon fish sauce

3 tablespoons oyster sauce

½ teaspoon chilli (red pepper) flakes

1 teaspoon cornflour (cornstarch)

60ml (¼ cup) cold water

Pork meatballs

500g (1lb 2oz) minced (ground) pork

1 tablespoon sesame oil

1 egg

2 tablespoons panko breadcrumbs

2 garlic cloves, peeled and minced

1 teaspoon minced ginger

1 lemongrass stalk, outer leaves removed, inner stalk very finely chopped (or 2 teaspoons lemongrass paste)

1 red chilli, finely chopped or ½ teaspoon chilli (red pepper) flakes

¼ teaspoon salt

¼ teaspoon white pepper

2 tablespoons finely chopped coriander stalks (the leaves are used in the sauce)

1   Place all the meatball ingredients into a large bowl and mix together with your hands. Form the mixture into walnut-size meatballs – you should get about 20 meatballs.

2   Heat the oil in a large frying pan (skillet) over a medium–high heat. Add the meatballs and brown on all sides – this should take 6–8 minutes.

3   Meanwhile, in a small bowl, mix together the soy sauce, lime juice, sugar, garlic, fish sauce, oyster sauce, chilli flakes, cornflour and water.

4   Pour the mixture into the pan with the meatballs. Allow to bubble for 2 minutes, then make a space in the centre of the pan and add the noodles. Toss the noodles in the sauce and cook for 2–3 minutes until the noodles are hot.

5   Stir through the coriander, then turn off the heat.

6   Divide the noodles between bowls and add the meatballs, then serve topped with a sprinkling of black sesame seeds.

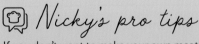 Nicky's pro tips

If you don't want to make your own meatballs, you can buy ready-made. Pork, turkey, chicken or beef meatballs all work with this recipe. You can add the lemongrass directly to the sauce, so you still get that lemongrass flavour.

Griddled lamb cutlets
with coriander pesto

££££

This recipe was inspired by a fantastic Indian restaurant I went to where it was served as a starter. The taste was amazing (if a little spicier than my version). This one has all the flavour, but without the heat. If you like the sound of the spicy version, though, sprinkle ½ teaspoon of cayenne pepper onto the lamb cutlets before cooking and add 1–2 jalapeños to the pesto before blending.

 Serves 4   Prep time 15 mins   Cook time 10 mins   Total time 25 mins

12 lamb cutlets (chops)
4 tablespoons oil
½ teaspoon salt
½ teaspoon ground black pepper
2 teaspoons dried oregano
2 teaspoons paprika
1 teaspoon garlic powder
1 batch Coriander pesto (page 197), made without jalapeños if preferred

To serve
steamed new potatoes
steamed peas

1   For the lamb, heat a large griddle pan (grill pan) over a high heat until hot. Brush the lamb cutlets with the oil, then sprinkle all over with the salt, pepper, oregano, paprika and garlic powder.

2   Place on the griddle and cook for 2–3 minutes on each side until well browned. You may need to work in two batches, depending on the size of your pan. If you do, then keep the first batch warm by placing on a board or tray and cover with a piece of foil and a tea towel (dish towel).

3   Once all the lamb cutlets are cooked, place on a board and cover with foil and a tea towel. Allow to rest for 3 minutes before serving, drizzled with coriander pesto. I like to serve this with steamed new potatoes and peas.

🗨 *Nicky's pro tips*

As tasty as they are, lamb cutlets are pretty small (about two bites per cutlet), so if you want more meat, add an extra cutlet or two per person.

Moreish Meat

Lamb kofta flatbreads with whipped feta

Juicy lamb kofta kebabs with a hint of warming spices. You can cook these on the griddle (grill pan) or barbecue, or under the grill (broiler). I love to serve them up on warm flatbreads with a creamy-yet-tangy feta dip, tomatoes and lots of crunchy red onions.

 Serves 4   Prep time 20 mins   Cook time 10 mins   Total time 30 mins

500g (1lb 2oz) minced (ground) lamb

3 tablespoons panko breadcrumbs

½ small onion, peeled and finely diced

2 garlic cloves, peeled and minced

1 teaspoon dried mint or 1 tablespoon finely chopped fresh mint

2 teaspoons ground cumin

1 teaspoon ground coriander

½ teaspoon salt

½ teaspoon ground black pepper

1 tablespoon oil

Whipped feta

200g (7oz) feta

100g (3½oz) cream cheese

1 small clove garlic, peeled and minced

3 tablespoons olive oil

1 teaspoon lemon juice

3 tablespoons cold water

To serve

4 Greek-style flatbreads, warmed in the oven or toaster

1 teaspoon chilli (red pepper) flakes

1 small red onion, peeled and finely sliced

10 cherry tomatoes, chopped into quarters

a small bunch of fresh flat-leaf parsley, roughly chopped

lemon wedges

1   Add the lamb, panko breadcrumbs, onion, garlic, mint, cumin, coriander, salt and pepper to a large bowl. Mix to combine, then divide the mixture into eight and mould each portion on wooden or metal skewers to form eight koftas.

2   Brush the koftas with the oil and heat a griddle pan (grill pan) over a medium–high heat. Alternatively, preheat the grill (broiler) to high and place a wire rack in the grill tray. Cook the koftas for 6–7 minutes, turning a few times during cooking, until well browned and cooked through.

3   While the koftas are cooking, make the whipped feta. Place the feta, cream cheese, garlic, oil, lemon juice and water into the bowl of a small food processor and blend together until smooth. If you would like a thinner consistency, add more oil or a splash of water. Transfer the whipped feta to a serving dish.

4   When the lamb koftas are cooked, remove from the heat and allow to rest for 2–3 minutes.

5   Serve the lamb koftas on warmed flatbreads, topped with the whipped feta, chilli flakes, red onion, tomatoes, parsley and lemon wedges.

Nicky's pro tips

If you're using wooden skewers for this recipe, ensure you soak the skewers in water for at least 30 minutes to ensure they don't burn during cooking.

Minute steak curry

Beef curries often take a long time to cook in order to ensure tender, fall-apart meat. However, this recipe uses strips of thin steak (a little goes a long way,) which lends itself perfectly to quick cooking – meaning you can have a beefy curry on the table in 25 minutes!

 Serves 4   **Prep time** 10 mins   **Cook time** 15 mins   **Total time** 25 mins

---

1 tablespoon oil
400g (14oz) minute, thin rib-eye or sirloin steak
¼ teaspoon salt
¼ teaspoon ground black pepper

Curry
1 tablespoon oil
1 onion, peeled and chopped into wedges
1 red (bell) pepper, deseeded and chopped into chunky pieces
12 cherry tomatoes, sliced in half (or 3–4 regular tomatoes, roughly chopped)
1 green chilli, finely chopped
3 garlic cloves, peeled and minced
2 teaspoons minced ginger

2 tablespoons mild curry powder (go hotter if you prefer)
1 tablespoon ground coriander
½ tablespoon ground cumin
1 teaspoon paprika
½ teaspoon ground cinnamon
½ teaspoon salt
½ teaspoon ground black pepper
1 x 400g (14oz) can finely chopped tomatoes
240g (1 cup) coconut cream

To serve
chopped fresh coriander (cilantro)
boiled rice
poppadoms

1. Start with the steak. Heat a large frying pan (skillet) over a high heat. Coat the steak in the oil and season on both sides with the salt and pepper. Add the steak to the hot pan. Fry for 1 minute each side, then remove from the pan and place, covered, on a plate.

2. Reduce the heat to medium (you'll be making the sauce in the same pan). Add the oil, then the onion, red pepper, tomatoes, chilli, garlic, ginger, curry powder, coriander, cumin, paprika, cinnamon, salt and pepper. Fry together, stirring constantly, for 4 minutes until the onion starts to soften.

3. Add the canned tomatoes and coconut cream. Stir again and bring to the boil, then reduce the heat and simmer for 5 minutes.

4. Meanwhile, cut the steak into thin slices.

5. Add the sliced steak back into the pan (along with any resting juices) and stir together. Simmer for a further 2 minutes, then turn off the heat and serve, topped with fresh coriander. I like to serve this with boiled rice and poppadoms.

Nicky's pro tips
If you can't get hold of coconut cream, place a can of coconut milk in the refrigerator for a couple of hours. Once chilled, open the can and spoon out the cream that will have solidified at the top of the can (there will be water-like liquid left in the can).

Moreish Meat

Steaky chips with peppercorn sauce

There's a café on the beach near where we live that sells the most amazing steaky chips. They're so good I had to figure out how to make them at home when the café closed for the winter season! I use frozen chips for this recipe, as I couldn't get it under 30 minutes when using homemade chips. You can make your own chips if you prefer and if you have a little more time to spare.

 Serves 4   Prep time 5 mins   Cook time 25 mins   Total time 30 mins

1kg (2lb 4oz) frozen oven chips
2 x 300g (10½oz) rib-eye steaks (removed from the refrigerator 30 minutes before cooking)
2 tablespoons oil
½ teaspoon salt
½ teaspoon ground black pepper

Peppercorn sauce
1 tablespoon unsalted butter
2 shallots, peeled and finely chopped
4 teaspoons black peppercorns, lightly crushed
¼ teaspoon salt
180ml (¾ cup) beef stock
1 teaspoon Worcestershire sauce
120ml (½ cup) double (heavy) cream
chopped fresh flat-leaf parsley, to serve

1. Start with the chips. Preheat the oven to 200–220°C fan/425–475°F/gas mark 7–9. Place the chips in a single layer on a large baking tray and cook as per the packet instructions (usually about 20–25 minutes).

2. When the chips have about 15 minutes left to cook, make the steak and peppercorn sauce. Heat a large frying pan (skillet) over a high heat.

3. Rub the oil into the steaks using your hands, then sprinkle the salt and pepper on both sides. Place the steaks in the pan and cook for 6 minutes, turning every minute. Remove from the pan and place, covered, on a plate to rest.

4. Add the butter to the pan you cooked the steaks in and reduce the heat to medium. When the butter has melted, add the shallots, peppercorns and salt and cook for 2–3 minutes until the shallots start to soften.

5. Add the stock and Worcestershire sauce and bring to the boil. Simmer rapidly for 5 minutes until reduced by half.

6. Pour in the cream and any resting juices from the steak and stir together.

7. Cut the steak into thin slices. Add to the sauce, stir together and turn off the heat.

8. Divide the chips between plates or bowls. Top with the steak strips and peppercorn sauce and serve sprinkled with fresh parsley.

Nicky's pro tips
This also works well as a centrepiece, served in one huge portion, on a tray, in the middle of the table. I like to serve it like this, alongside a big salad, so everyone can tuck in and add to their own plates with a set of tongs.

Crispy orange beef

£££

We're using steak for this recipe, which is a little bit extravagant, but it means we're getting tender meat, cooked in extra-quick time. I love the tanginess of the sauce, which soaks into the rice beautifully, meaning lots of flavour in every bite!

 Serves 4   **Prep time** 10 mins   **Cook time** 15 mins   **Total time** 25 mins

3 tablespoons oil

500g (1lb 2oz) steak (I use sirloin), sliced into strips (see Tip)

2 tablespoons cornflour (cornstarch)

a pinch of salt and pepper

1 red (bell) pepper, deseeded and sliced

1 large onion, peeled and sliced

zest of ½ orange

120ml (½ cup) orange juice (approx. juice of 2 large oranges)

5 tablespoons soy sauce

3 tablespoons caster (superfine) sugar

2 garlic cloves, peeled and crushed

1 teaspoon rice vinegar

1 teaspoon ginger paste

1 tablespoon cornflour (cornstarch), mixed with 3 tablespoons cold water to form a slurry (optional)

To serve

boiled rice

4 spring onions (scallions), chopped on the diagonal

1   Heat the oil in a wok or large frying pan (skillet) over a high heat.

2   Pat the beef dry with kitchen paper, then mix the cornflour with the salt and pepper and toss the beef in the cornflour until completely coated.

3   When the oil is hot, tip the beef in and spread it out. Fry until crispy. Try not to move the meat around too much as this reduces the amount of crispiness you get. It should take 5–6 minutes to crisp up the beef, with about three or four stirs during that time.

4   Once the beef is crispy and cooked through, remove the slices using a slotted spoon and place in a bowl lined with kitchen paper to soak up excess oil.

5   There should still be a little oil left in the pan. Reduce the heat to medium and add the red pepper and onion. Fry for 2–3 minutes – you want them hot but still crunchy.

6   While the peppers and onions are cooking, mix the orange zest, juice, soy sauce, sugar, garlic, rice vinegar and ginger in a small bowl.

7   Pour the orange sauce into the pan. Increase the heat and bring to the boil. Simmer for 1 minute.

8   Then add the beef back in. Give it a stir and heat through for 1 minute. If your sauce is looking too thin, you can stir in a little cornflour slurry to thicken it.

9   Once bubbling and thick, serve with boiled rice. Garnish with the spring onions.

💬 *Nicky's pro tips*

It's easier to slice the raw steak into thin strips if you place it in the freezer for 10 minutes to firm up a little first.

Quick chilli con carne

Get all those fantastic chilli con carne flavours in a quarter of the time. We're stretching a small pack of minced (ground) beef to serve four people, which makes this a great budget-conscious, yet filling and tasty meal.

 Serves 4   **Prep time** 10 mins   **Cook time** 20 mins   **Total time** 30 mins

2 tablespoons oil
1 onion, peeled and finely diced
250g (9oz) minced (ground) beef (10–15% fat)
½ teaspoon salt
½ teaspoon ground black pepper
3 garlic cloves, peeled and minced
1 teaspoon ground ginger
1 teaspoon ground cumin
1 beef stock (bouillon) cube, crumbled
1 teaspoon smoked paprika
1 teaspoon ground coriander
½ teaspoon chilli powder
2 tablespoons tomato purée (paste)
1 x 400g (14oz) can chopped tomatoes
1 x 400g (14oz) can mixed beans in chilli sauce
½ teaspoon chipotle paste
1 tablespoon tomato ketchup
1 tablespoon light brown sugar
1 tablespoon Worcestershire sauce
1 teaspoon dried coriander leaf

To serve
boiled rice
chopped fresh coriander (cilantro)

1   Add the oil to a frying pan (skillet) over a medium–high heat. Add the onion, beef, salt and pepper and cook for 5 minutes until the beef is browned and the onion has started to soften.

2   Add the garlic, ginger, cumin, beef stock cube, paprika, ground coriander, chilli powder and tomato purée and cook for another 30 seconds, stirring constantly.

3   Add the canned tomatoes, mixed beans, chipotle paste, ketchup, sugar, Worcestershire sauce and dried coriander. Stir everything together, bring to a simmer and cook for 10–15 minutes, stirring occasionally.

4   Serve over boiled rice, topped with a sprinkling of fresh coriander.

Nicky's pro tips

This is one of those meals that tastes even better the next day, so it's great for making ahead. Make the chilli, then cool, cover and refrigerate. Reheat in a saucepan, stirring often, until piping hot throughout. You can add a splash of water or stock to loosen it up if needed.

Minced beef & potatoes

Being a Northern lass, this, to me, is the epitome of a stick-to-your-ribs, tasty, filling dinner. It's simple and hearty, and that's what I love about it.

 Serves 4   Prep time 5 mins   Cook time 25 mins   Total time 30 mins

1 tablespoon oil
1 large onion, peeled and chopped
1 celery stick, finely chopped
1 carrot, peeled and finely chopped
450g (1lb) minced (ground) beef
1 teaspoon salt
1 teaspoon ground black pepper
1 tablespoon Worcestershire sauce
480ml (2 cups) beef stock
2 tablespoons cornflour (cornstarch), mixed with 6 tablespoons cold water to form a slurry

Potatoes
750g (1lb 10oz) baby new potatoes (halve any that are larger than a golf ball)
2 tablespoons salted butter
1 teaspoon dried parsley (or 1 tablespoon finely chopped fresh parsley)
a pinch of salt and pepper

To serve
green vegetables, such as peas
pickled red cabbage

1. Start by cooking the potatoes. Place the potatoes in a large saucepan and cover with cold water. Bring to the boil, then simmer for 15–20 minutes until the potatoes are tender (you can check this by slicing into a potato with a knife – it should slide in easily). Drain.

2. While the potatoes are cooking, add the oil to a large frying pan (skillet) over a medium–high heat.

3. Add the onion, celery and carrot and cook for 5 minutes, stirring often, until slightly softened.

4. Add the beef, salt and pepper. Increase the heat to high and cook for 5 minutes, stirring often (breaking up any large lumps as you go), until browned.

5. Add the Worcestershire sauce and beef stock. Bring to the boil, then simmer for 5–6 minutes until slightly reduced.

6. Stir in the cornflour slurry until the liquid has thickened to your liking. Then turn off the heat.

7. By now the potatoes should be cooked and drained. Place in a bowl with the butter and parsley, plus the salt and pepper and stir together, ensuring the butter and parsley coats the potatoes.

8. Divide the potatoes and beef between plates or bowls. I like to serve mine with peas and pickled red cabbage.

Nicky's pro tips
Use 12–15% fat beef, rather than very low fat. The extra fat keeps the beef juicy and gives it more flavour when frying.

Perfect
Pasta

I'm a serious pasta lover. In fact, I think it would be one of my three desert island essentials.

In this chapter, we've got pasta recipes that include lots of delicious goodies – like bacon, peas, chorizo and garlic chicken.

We've also got a couple of really simple recipes, such as my **Garlic bread spaghetti** (see page 121) and **Chilli oil spaghetti** (see page 118), which both have a short ingredients list, but still provide ultimate taste satisfaction. And all of them are ready and on the table in 30 minutes or less!

If you've never tried orzo, which is a rice-shaped pasta that soaks up lots of flavour and cooks very quickly, then start with my **Tomato and sausage orzo** with olives, capers and rocket (aragula) on page 134. It'll really make your taste buds tingle!

£

Chilli oil spaghetti

It looks simple, it IS simple, but it tastes amazing. Al dente pasta is tossed in warm garlicky olive oil with chilli flakes for some gentle warming heat.

 Serves
4

Prep time
2 mins

 Cook time
15 mins

 Total time
17 mins

400g (14oz) spaghetti
5 tablespoons extra virgin olive oil
1 teaspoon chilli (red pepper) flakes
3 garlic cloves, peeled and minced
½ teaspoon salt
½ teaspoon ground black pepper
3 tablespoons finely chopped
   fresh flat-leaf parsley

To serve
4 tablespoons shaved vegetarian
   Italian-style hard cheese (or
   Parmesan for non-vegetarians)
ground black pepper

1 Cook the spaghetti in boiling salted water, as per the packet instructions (ideally until al dente – usually 8–10 minutes). Once cooked, drain, reserving ½ cup of the cooking water.

2 When the pasta is almost cooked (about 5 minutes from the end of cooking), heat the oil in a large frying pan (skillet) over a low–medium heat. Add the chilli flakes, garlic, salt and pepper. Fry for 3–4 minutes, stirring often.

3 Add the drained spaghetti and a good splash (about 4 tablespoons) of pasta cooking water. Stir together, adding more pasta water, if desired. Then stir in the chopped parsley.

4 Divide between bowls and top with shaved cheese and black pepper.

Nicky's pro tips.
If you want a little cheesy creaminess, add 2–3 tablespoons of grated (shredded) vegetarian Italian-style hard cheese (or Parmesan) at the same time you add the cooked pasta to the frying pan.

Garlic bread spaghetti

£

If you've never blitzed a garlic baguette and then toasted the resulting breadcrumbs, you don't know what you're missing! Those golden, crispy, garlic-bread crumbs are tossed together with spaghetti, plus a hint of chilli and lemon. A revelation of a dinner, ready in 20 minutes!

 Serves 4   **Prep time** 5 mins   **Cook time** 15 mins   **Total time** 20 mins

300g (10½oz) spaghetti
1 x part-baked garlic baguette (about 200g/7oz), chilled (not frozen)
2 tablespoons olive oil
1 red chilli, finely chopped
zest and juice of ½ lemon
50g (½ cup) finely grated (shredded) vegetarian Italian-style hard cheese (or use Parmesan for non-vegetarians), plus extra to serve
2 tablespoons chopped fresh flat-leaf parsley
¼ teaspoon salt
¼ teaspoon ground black pepper

To serve
lemon zest
ground black pepper

1 Cook the spaghetti in boiling salted water, as per the packet instructions– usually about 12 minutes.

2 While the spaghetti is cooking, rip the garlic baguette into large chunks and pulse in a food processor until you have rough breadcrumbs.

3 Heat 1½ tablespoons of the olive oil in a large frying pan (skillet) and fry the garlic breadcrumbs for 3–4 minutes until golden brown. Make sure you stir regularly to stop the breadcrumbs from burning. Remove from the pan and place on a plate.

4 Just before the spaghetti is ready, heat the remaining ½ tablespoon of oil in the pan and add the chopped chilli. Fry over a low–medium heat for 1–2 minutes.

5 Drain the spaghetti, reserving a cup of the cooking water.

6 Put the spaghetti in the frying pan along with 4 tablespoons of the pasta cooking water.

7 Add the lemon zest and juice, cheese, parsley, salt and pepper. Toss to combine. Add a little more cooking water if you want the dish to be a little creamier.

8 Stir through three-quarters of the breadcrumbs, then divide between bowls. Top with the rest of the garlic breadcrumbs, plus a sprinkling of grated cheese, lemon zest and black pepper.

 Nicky's pro tips

Garlic bread can sometimes be salty, or not salty at all, depending on the brand you use. This recipe assumes you're using seasoned/salty garlic bread. If you're not (or you're not sure), have a taste of the garlic breadcrumbs when you've fried them. Add a good pinch of salt to the crumbs if you think they need it.

Perfect Pasta

One-pan chicken & broccoli pasta

A throw-it-all-in-the pan weeknight meal that ticks the meat/carb/vegetable boxes with minimal effort. It's a nice light recipe, which gives this meal a bit of a summery vibe. If you want it creamier, you can double the Parmesan and add in a splash of double (heavy) cream.

 Serves 4   **Prep time** 5 mins   **Cook time** 25 mins   **Total time** 30 mins

2 tablespoons olive oil
1 small onion, peeled and diced
3 chicken breasts (about 525g/1lb 3oz), chopped into bite-size chunks
¼ teaspoon salt
¼ teaspoon ground black pepper
3 garlic cloves, peeled and minced
60ml (¼ cup) white wine
600ml (2½ cups) good-quality chicken stock
180ml (¾ cup) full-fat (whole) milk
300g (10½oz) pasta shapes (I use fusilli)
300g (10½oz) head of broccoli, stalk removed and chopped into small florets
1 teaspoon lemon juice
50g (½ packed cup) grated (shredded) Parmesan

To serve
chopped fresh flat-leaf parsley
ground black pepper

1   Heat the oil in a deep-sided, heavy-based pan over a medium–high heat. Add the onion, chicken, salt and pepper and fry for 5–6 minutes until the onion starts to become translucent.

2   Add the garlic, stir and cook for 30 seconds. Pour in the wine and bring to the boil. Simmer for 1–2 minutes, then add the stock and milk.

3   Bring to the boil, then stir in the pasta. Bring back to a gentle bubble and place a lid on the pan. Reduce the heat and cook for 10 minutes.

4   Add the broccoli, stir, place the lid back on and cook for another 5 minutes until the broccoli is tender and the pasta is cooked.

5   Remove the lid and stir in the lemon juice and Parmesan.

6   Serve, topped with a sprinkling of parsley and black pepper.

> *Nicky's pro tips*
>
> If you want to add in extra vegetables, mushrooms and chopped kale or spinach make great additions. Add mushrooms just before you add the wine and add kale/spinach during the last 5 minutes of cooking.

Garlic & Parmesan chicken linguine

All made in one pan, this chicken linguine is creamy, rich and luscious! It's one of those perfect bowl-food comfort dinners to eat on the sofa in front of the TV, but it works equally well as an indulgent date-night dinner.

 Serves 4   **Prep time** 10 mins   **Cook time** 20 mins   **Total time** 30 mins

2 tablespoons olive oil

2 large chicken breasts (about 200g/7oz each), butterflied

½ teaspoon salt

½ teaspoon ground black pepper, plus extra to serve

1 tablespoon unsalted butter

4 garlic cloves, peeled and minced

480ml (2 cups) chicken stock

240ml (1 cup) full-fat (whole) milk

300g (10½oz) linguine

60ml (¼ cup) double (heavy) cream

50g (½ packed cup) grated (shredded) Parmesan

2 tablespoons finely chopped fresh flat-leaf parsley

1. Heat the oil in a large frying pan (skillet) over a medium–high heat. Sprinkle the chicken breasts with the salt and pepper and place in the pan. Fry for 5–6 minutes, turning once, until golden and cooked throughout (so the chicken is no longer pink in the middle).

2. Remove the chicken from the pan and place on a chopping board.

3. Reduce the heat to medium. Add the butter to the pan and heat until the butter melts.

4. Add the garlic and stir together for 30 seconds. Add the chicken stock and milk, stir together and bring to the boil.

5. Add the linguine, stir, ensuring all of the linguine is covered in liquid. Bring to a simmer, place a lid on the pan and simmer for 10–12 minutes until the linguine is cooked through. Check a couple of times and use a set of tongs to separate the linguine strands if it looks like they are sticking at all.

6. Remove the lid and stir in the cream and Parmesan.

7. Slice the cooked chicken into strips and add to the pan, along with the chopped parsley. Stir together and heat through for another minute.

8. Turn off the heat and divide between bowls. Top with a little black pepper before serving.

🗨️ *Nicky's pro tips*

I like to serve this dish alongside a salad or some steamed vegetables, but you can also cook vegetables in the pan with the linguine if you like. Add small florets of broccoli, chopped green beans, fine asparagus, or frozen peas to the pan for the last 6–7 minutes of cooking.

Perfect Pasta

BBQ chicken pasta

This is a simple pasta dish with a delicious smokiness from the BBQ sauce. I love the creamy mild flavour of the red Leicester cheese and the saltiness of the crispy bacon. I counterbalance the distinct lack of veg in this dish by serving it with a huge crispy green salad.

 Serves 4   Prep time 5 mins   Cook time 20 mins   Total time 25 mins

300g (10½oz) pasta shapes (I use spirali)
1 tablespoon oil
4 rashers (strips) streaky bacon
1 onion, peeled and chopped
2 chicken breasts (about 350g/12oz), chopped into bite-size pieces
⅛ teaspoon salt
⅛ teaspoon ground black pepper
2 garlic cloves, peeled and minced
1 x 400g (14oz) can finely chopped tomatoes
1 tablespoon tomato purée (paste)
80ml (⅓ cup) barbecue sauce

To serve
50g (½ packed cup) grated red Leicester cheese (or Cheddar if preferred)
2 tablespoons chopped chives

1   Cook the pasta in boiling salted water, as per the packet instructions. Drain, reserving ½ cup of the cooking water.

2   Meanwhile, heat the oil in a large frying pan (skillet) over a medium–high heat. Add the bacon and cook for 5–6 minutes, turning once, until browned and crispy. Remove from the pan and place on a chopping board. Roughly slice the bacon and set aside.

3   In the same pan you cooked the bacon, add the onion, chicken, salt and pepper. Cook for 5 minutes, stirring often, until the chicken is sealed and the onion starts to soften.

4   Stir in the garlic, then add the canned tomatoes, tomato purée and barbecue sauce. Stir together and bring to the boil. Simmer for 5–6 minutes, stirring occasionally, until the chicken is cooked through.

5   Add the cooked pasta to the frying pan and stir together. Add splashes of the pasta cooking water if you want to loosen the sauce further.

6   Turn off the heat, then sprinkle on the crispy bacon and grated red Leicester.

7   Place under the grill (broiler) for 1–2 minutes until the cheese is melted (make sure your pan is grillproof).

8   Sprinkle over the chives and serve.

Nicky's pro tips

If you don't want to place the pan under the grill, place a lid on the pan after adding the cheese and cook for another minute to melt the cheese. Then top with the chives and serve.

Easy orzo with tomato and crispy bacon

££

Orzo is so underrated! It makes a brilliant alternative to risotto and you can cook it directly in your sauce, meaning it absorbs all the lovely flavour! The bacon, sun-blushed tomatoes and crumbled chunks of Cheddar all add little zings of flavour when you're eating it too. So tasty!

 Serves 4

Prep time 5 mins

 Cook time 25 mins

 Total time 30 mins

1 tablespoon oil
200g (7oz) bacon rashers (strips)
2 garlic cloves, peeled and minced
1 x 400g (14oz) can finely chopped tomatoes
360ml (1½ cups) chicken stock
200g (7oz) orzo
1 tablespoon tomato purée (paste)
½ teaspoon salt
½ teaspoon ground black pepper
100g (3½oz) baby spinach
250g (9oz) sun-blushed/ sun-soaked tomatoes in oil, drained
100g (3½oz) Cheddar, crumbled

1. Heat the oil in a large frying pan (skillet) over a medium–high heat. Add the bacon and fry for 5–6 minutes until crispy. Remove from the pan, leaving the oil behind. Reduce the heat to low.

2. Add the garlic and fry for 30 seconds, then add the canned tomatoes, stock, orzo, tomato purée, salt and pepper. Stir together and bring to the boil. Reduce to a simmer, place a lid on and cook for 12–14 minutes, stirring occasionally, until the orzo is cooked through.

3. While the orzo is cooking, chop the bacon into small pieces.

4. When the orzo is cooked, remove the lid and stir through the spinach, sun-blushed tomatoes and cooked bacon. Sprinkle the crumbled Cheddar on top and serve.

Nicky's pro tips

Be sure to give the orzo a good stir a few times during cooking. It takes a little longer to cook in the sauce than it would in water and you need to stir it to ensure it cooks evenly and doesn't catch on the bottom of the pan.

Make it vegetarian

Swap out the bacon for chopped up vegetarian sausages or a vegetarian-style bacon alternative. Swap the chicken stock for vegetable stock.

Perfect Pasta

Spicy tomato & chorizo bucatini

This is a simple, spicy tomato pasta dish with a bit of a nod towards the classic Italian dish Pasta Amatriciana, which uses guanciale and Pecorino rather than the chorizo and Parmesan I use in this recipe.

 Serves 4   **Prep time** 10 mins   **Cook time** 20 mins   **Total time** 30 mins

1 tablespoon olive oil

200g (7oz) chorizo, chopped into small chunks

300g (10½oz) bucatini

1 onion, peeled and finely chopped

¼ teaspoon salt

½ teaspoon ground black pepper

2 garlic cloves, peeled and minced

1 teaspoon chilli (red pepper) flakes

2 tablespoons tomato purée (paste)

1 x 400g (14oz) can finely chopped tomatoes

120ml (½ cup) chicken stock

50g (½ cup) grated (shredded) Parmesan

To serve

a small bunch of flat-leaf parsley, finely chopped

grated Parmesan

ground black pepper

1   Put a large pan of salted water on to boil for the pasta.

2   Meanwhile, heat the oil in a large frying pan (skillet) over a medium heat. Add the chorizo and cook for 5–6 minutes, stirring often, until lightly browned and slightly crisp. Remove from the pan with a slotted spoon and place in a bowl. There will be oil left in the pan from cooking the chorizo.

3   By now the water for the pasta should be boiling. Cook the bucatini, as per the packet instructions (usually about 10 minutes). Once cooked, drain, reserving a cup of the cooking water.

4   Meanwhile, add the onion, salt and pepper to the frying pan with the chorizo oil and cook for 5 minutes, stirring often, until the onion starts to soften.

5   Add the garlic, chilli flakes and tomato purée. Cook for a further 2 minutes, stirring.

6   Add the canned tomatoes and stock. Bring to the boil and then simmer for 5 minutes.

7   Add the cooked chorizo back to the frying pan, along with the drained bucatini and Parmesan. Stir together and heat for another 2 minutes. Add splashes of the pasta cooking water if you want to loosen the sauce.

8   Divide the pasta between bowls and top with chopped parsley, Parmesan and black pepper before serving.

💬 *Nicky's pro tips*

Swap out the bucatini for your favourite pasta. Tagliatelle or linguine work really well.

Creamy bacon & pea pasta

££

Salty bacon and sweet peas are such a great combination in this ultra-simple pasta dish. Most of the recipe is made while the pasta is cooking, with just a couple of extra steps at the end to bring it all together. Perfect when you need to get dinner on the table quickly, without faffing around with lots of ingredients!

 Serves 4   **Prep time** 5 mins   **Cook time** 20 mins   **Total time** 25 mins

400g (14oz) pasta shells
1 tablespoon oil
160g (5¾oz) bacon lardons
1 onion, peeled and finely diced
2 garlic cloves, peeled and minced
1 chicken stock (bouillon) cube, crumbled
120ml (½ cup) double (heavy) cream
150g (1 cup) frozen peas
75g (¾ packed cup) grated (shredded) Parmesan

To serve
chopped fresh flat-leaf parsley
black pepper

1. Cook the pasta shells in boiling salted water for 1 minute less than the packet instructions. Drain, reserving a cup of the cooking water.

2. While the pasta is cooking, heat the oil in a large frying pan (skillet) over a medium heat. Add the bacon lardons and fry for 5–6 minutes, stirring occasionally, until golden. Remove from the pan with slotted spoon and place in a bowl.

3. Add the onion to the pan and cook for 3–4 minutes, stirring often, until soft. Add the garlic and cook for a further minute.

4. Stir the chicken stock cube into the reserved cup of pasta cooking water.

5. Add the pasta to the pan and half the stock-flavoured cooking water. Add the cream and peas and heat, stirring often, for 2 minutes.

6. Stir in the Parmesan. Add more of the water if you want to loosen the sauce at all.

7. Add the cooked bacon lardons back to the pan and cook for a further 1–2 minutes until the peas and bacon are hot.

8. Serve topped with fresh parsley and black pepper.

🗨️ Nicky's pro tips

If you want to add in some more vegetables, baby spinach and chopped cherry tomatoes can be stirred in during the last minute, along with the cooked bacon.

🍳 Make it vegetarian

Swap out the bacon lardons for chopped vegetarian sausages or a vegetarian-style bacon alternative. Swap the chicken stock cube for a vegetable one. The Parmesan can also be swapped for vegetarian Italian-style hard cheese.

Perfect Pasta

Tomato & sausage orzo

This flavourful dinner has got a bit of Spanish-Italian feel to it with the addition of tomatoes, olives and capers to the little bites of orzo pasta. I like to use flavoured pork sausages, but you can use regular pork, chicken or vegetarian sausages.

 Serves 4   Prep time 10 mins   Cook time 20 mins   Total time 30 mins

6 medium pork sausages
   (flavoured or plain – see Tip)
1 tablespoon oil
1 onion, peeled and diced
1 red (bell) pepper, deseeded and
   thinly sliced
1 green (bell) pepper, deseeded
   and thinly sliced
2 garlic cloves, peeled and minced
1 teaspoon chilli powder (mild or
   hot, depending on your
   preference)
2 teaspoons smoked paprika
½ teaspoon salt
½ teaspoon ground black pepper
1 tablespoon tomato purée (paste)
1 x 400g (14oz) can finely
   chopped tomatoes
360ml (1½ cups) chicken stock
200g (7oz) orzo
100g (3½oz) mixed olives, pitted
   and sliced in half
1 tablespoon capers, drained
12 cherry tomatoes, sliced in half
50g (2 packed cups) mild rocket
   (arugula) or lamb's lettuce

1. Place the sausages on a grill tray and place under the grill (broiler) for 20 minutes, turning regularly, until browned all over and cooked through. Alternatively, if you have an air fryer, they can be air-fried at 200°C/400°F for 10–12 minutes.

2. Meanwhile, heat the oil in a large frying pan (skillet) over a medium heat. Add the onion and red and green peppers. Cook for 4–5 minutes, stirring regularly, until the onion starts to soften.

3. Add the garlic, chilli powder, smoked paprika, salt, pepper and tomato purée to the pan and stir together for 1 minute.

4. Add the canned tomatoes and chicken stock, stir and bring to the boil, then add the orzo. Stir together, then add the olives, capers and cherry tomatoes.

5. Reduce the heat, so the liquid is simmering very gently, place a lid on and cook for 10 minutes, stirring occasionally, until the orzo is cooked.

6. By now, the sausages should be cooked. Place them on a chopping board and cut into thick slices.

7. Remove the lid from the pan, then stir in the sliced sausages and rocket – it should wilt a little as you stir it in.

8. Divide between bowls and serve.

Nicky's pro tips

Plain pork sausages work well in this dish, but sometimes I like to change it up using flavoured sausages. Spicy/chilli sausage, black pepper sausage and Italian-herb sausage all work well.

Make it vegetarian

Replace the pork sausages with vegetarian sausages and swap the chicken stock for vegetable stock.

Pancetta carbonara

££

A classic carbonara doesn't need cream in order to get that traditional creamy texture. The eggs, cheese, starchy pasta water and fat from cooking the pancetta are the magic ingredients for a rich, glossy, creamy sauce. Be sure to turn the heat off before adding the eggs and the sauce will come together beautifully with no risk of scrambling.

 Serves 4   **Prep time** 10 mins   **Cook time** 10 mins   **Total time** 20 mins

400g (14oz) spaghetti

3 large eggs

50g (½ cup) finely grated (shredded) Pecorino Romano or Grana Padano (or just use extra Parmesan)

50g (½ cup) finely grated Parmesan

1 tablespoon olive oil

200g (7oz) pancetta cubes

2 garlic cloves, peeled and minced

¼ teaspoon salt

½ teaspoon ground black pepper

To serve

chopped fresh flat-leaf parsley

ground black pepper

1. Cook the pasta in boiling salted water, as per the packet instructions.

2. Mix the eggs in a bowl together with the Pecorino Romano and half the Parmesan. Set aside.

3. After the pasta has been cooking for 5 minutes, heat the oil in a large frying pan (skillet) over a medium heat. Add the pancetta and fry for 3–4 minutes until starting to crisp up, then add the garlic and cook for a further 30 seconds.

4. By now, the pasta should be ready (if it's not, turn off the heat under the pan with the pancetta and reheat it for a few seconds when ready). Using tongs, remove the pasta from the water (reserving the water in the pan) and transfer to the pan with the pancetta. Add the salt and pepper.

5. Toss the spaghetti in the pan over the heat for a minute, then turn off the heat.

6. Add 4 tablespoons of the reserved pasta water to the pan, then while constantly lifting and lowering the pasta with the tongs, pour the egg mixture into the pan with the pasta.

7. Continue lifting and lowering until the egg mixture coats the pasta. Add a little more pasta water if needed, until you have a lovely creamy sauce.

8. Divide the pasta between bowls and top with the remaining Parmesan. Sprinkle on the parsley and black pepper before serving.

Nicky's pro tips

The pancetta can be replaced by the beautifully rich and fatty guanciale, which is more traditional in carbonara. Or you could replace with chopped streaky bacon.

Perfect Pasta

One-pan spaghetti & meatballs

££

The meatballs are juicy with a light crust and the spaghetti absorbs so much flavour while it cooks in the tomato ragù. This is a winning dinner with minimal washing up!

 Serves
4

 Prep time
10 mins

 Cook time
20 mins

 Total time
30 mins

500g (1lb 2oz) minced (ground) beef
½ large onion, peeled and finely chopped
1 egg
3 tablespoons grated (shredded) Parmesan, plus extra to serve
3 tablespoons panko breadcrumbs
¼ teaspoon salt
¼ teaspoon ground black pewpper
1 tablespoon oil
1 tablespoon unsalted butter
200g (7oz) spaghetti
1 tablespoon chopped fresh flat-leaf parsley, to serve

Sauce
½ large onion, peeled and finely chopped
2 celery sticks, chopped
2 garlic cloves, peeled and minced
¼ teaspoon salt
¼ teaspoon ground black pepper
1 x 400g (14oz) can finely chopped tomatoes
2 tablespoons tomato purée (paste)
1 teaspoon dried thyme
1 teaspoon light brown sugar
1 beef stock (bouillon) cube, crumbled
600ml (2½ cups) just-boiled water

1 Put the beef, onion, egg, Parmesan, breadcrumbs, salt and pepper in a large bowl. Mix together using your hands, then form the mixture into 16–20 meatballs.

2 Heat the oil and butter in a large frying pan (skillet) and add the meatballs. Cook over a medium–high heat for 5–6 minutes, turning two or three times, until the meatballs are browned all over. They don't need to be fully cooked at this point, as they'll cook further in the sauce.

3 Move the meatballs to one side of the pan (or just make a bit of a space). Add the onion, celery, garlic, salt and pepper. Cook for 3–4 minutes, stirring the vegetables a few times, until the onion starts to soften.

4 Add the canned tomatoes, tomato purée, thyme, sugar, crumbled stock cube and the just-boiled water. Stir together and bring to the boil.

5 Add the pasta (break in half if it's too big to fit in your pan). Ensure the pasta is fully submerged in the sauce. Reduce the heat to low, place a lid on and cook for 10–12 minutes, stirring a couple of times, until the pasta is cooked. Separate the pasta with a set of tongs to stop it sticking together. Add another splash of boiling water during cooking, if required.

6 When the pasta is cooked, turn off the heat and divide the spaghetti between bowls, using the tongs. Spoon the meatballs and sauce on top.

7 Finish with a little Parmesan and chopped parsley and serve.

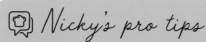 Nicky's pro tips

I prefer using a higher fat mince, such as 12–20% for more flavour.

Want to change it up?

- Add 1 teaspoon of chilli (red pepper) flakes or 1 tablespoon of sriracha to the sauce for a spicy version.

- Add 4 tablespoons of double (heavy) cream to the sauce, once the pasta is cooked, for a creamy tomato version.

- Top the finished dish with halved cherry tomatoes, a drizzle of pesto and some basil leaves for a fresh summer variation.

Quick & Easy

Make it vegetarian

Skip the chorizo entirely (if you do, add 1 teaspoon of smoked paprika with the spices), or replace it with vegetarian chorizo, mushrooms or smoky chickpeas (chickpeas fried with smoked paprika, cumin, salt and pepper). You'll also need to replace the Parmesan with vegetarian Italian-style hard cheese and check you're using a vegetarian mozzarella.

Penne arrabbiata with mozzarella & chorizo

££

A quick version of warming arrabbiata sauce, with pasta, slices of delicious fried chorizo and little nuggets of melty mozzarella. This dish ticks all the boxes for a satisfying, moreish dinner. I love it served with a big green salad.

Serves 4 | **Prep time** 10 mins | **Cook time** 20 mins | **Total time** 30 mins

1 red (bell) pepper
1 yellow (bell) pepper
400g (14oz) penne
1 tablespoon olive oil
1 onion, peeled and chopped
200g (7oz) chorizo, sliced
2 garlic cloves, peeled and minced
1 tablespoon tomato purée (paste)
1 x 400g (14oz) can chopped
    tomatoes
1 teaspoon dried thyme
1 heaped teaspoon chilli (red
    pepper) flakes
1 teaspoon sugar
250g (9oz) mozzarella, roughly torn

To serve

3 tablespoons finely grated
    (shredded) Parmesan
½ teaspoon ground black pepper
a pinch of chilli (red pepper) flakes
2 spring onions (scallions), sliced

1   Place the whole peppers on a grill tray and place under the grill (broiler). Grill until blackened and charred all over. Turn during grilling to ensure all the sides are charred. They should be blackened in 10–12 minutes.

2   Once blackened, wrap the peppers in foil and allow to cool slightly (this will make removing the skin easier).

3   While the peppers are grilling, cook the pasta in boiling salted water, as per the packet instructions.

4   Heat the oil in a large frying pan (skillet) and add the onion. Cook over a medium heat, stirring occasionally, for 2–3 minutes until the onion starts to soften.

5   Add the chorizo and cook for a further 3–4 minutes until it releases its oils and starts to darken.

6   Now stir in the garlic and tomato purée, cook for 1 minute, then stir in the canned tomatoes, thyme, chilli flakes and sugar. Bring it to a gentle bubble and simmer for 10 minutes.

7   By now, the foil-wrapped peppers should have cooled a little. Place them on a chopping board, then remove and discard the charred skin. Slice the peppers (discarding the seeds) and add them to the sauce.

8   Once cooked, drain the pasta and add it to the arrabbiata sauce. Stir together until the pasta is completely coated in the sauce.

9   Stir in the mozzarella, cook for 1 minute and then turn off the heat.

10 Sprinkle the arrabbiata with a little Parmesan, freshly ground black pepper, chilli flakes and some chopped spring onions. Serve straight from the pan.

Nicky's pro tips

I like to save some of this for an easy pasta salad lunch the next day. It tastes great cold, with some crunchy salad leaves and finely sliced red onion.

Perfect Pasta

One-pan minced beef macaroni

This is similar to a bolognese-style mac 'n' cheese, a bit more on the tomatoey side, rather than the creamy cheesiness of a regular mac 'n' cheese. However, there's still a nice hefty amount of cheese in there, so we're not missing out!

 Serves 4   **Prep time** 5 mins   **Cook time** 25 mins   **Total time** 30 mins

1 onion, peeled and roughly chopped
1 celery stick, roughly chopped
1 carrot, peeled and roughly chopped
3 garlic cloves, peeled
2 tablespoons olive oil
500g (1lb 2oz) minced (ground) beef
½ teaspoon salt
½ teaspoon ground black pepper, plus extra to serve
2 tablespoons tomato purée (paste)
300g (10½oz) macaroni
1 teaspoon dried oregano
½ tablespoon Worcestershire sauce
2 x 400g (14oz) cans finely chopped tomatoes
360ml (1½ cups) beef stock
120ml (½ cup) full-fat (whole) milk
200g (2 packed cups) mixed grated (shredded) cheese (I use Cheddar and red Leicester)

To serve
2 tablespoons chopped fresh flat-leaf parsley

1   Place the onion, celery, carrot and garlic in a food processor and pulse until finely chopped.

2   Heat the oil in a large frying pan (skillet) over a high heat. Add the vegetable mix, beef, salt and pepper and fry for 5 minutes, stirring often, until the beef is lightly browned.

3   Stir in the tomato purée, then add the macaroni, oregano, Worcestershire sauce, canned tomatoes, beef stock and milk. Stir together and bring to the boil, then put a lid on and simmer gently for 12–14 minutes, stirring occasionally, until the macaroni is tender.

4   Remove the lid and stir in half the cheese. Sprinkle the remaining cheese on top, cover with the lid again and cook for a further minute until the cheese melts.

5   Remove the lid, sprinkle on the fresh parsley and a little black pepper and serve.

💬 *Nicky's pro tips*

If you want to crisp up the cheese, place the pan under the grill (broiler) for 4–5 minutes until golden and bubbly. Make sure your pan is suitable for using under the grill.

Rice, Noodles, Grains & Pulses

Super-versatile, cost-effective, nutritious, tasty and filling – using rice, noodles, grains and pulses as the basis of a meal doesn't have to be bland and boring. I love these types of recipes so much that, despite dishes with these ingredients appearing elsewhere within this book, I felt they also deserved a chapter of their own.

My **Peanut butter ramen with beef** (see page 162) is a ridiculously quick dinner that uses a couple of tricks you may be surprised about, but trust me, the flavour is all there!

And the **Spicy bean tacos with feta** (see page 150)? No one says a word about the lack of meat as they're going in for seconds.

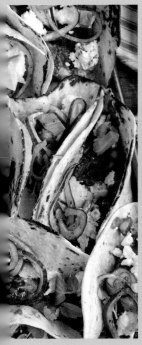  

Chickpea fritters

Canned chickpeas make a great base for crispy fritters. Plus they're inexpensive too! Adding spices, garlic and Parmesan gives them plenty of flavour. I like to serve mine with sweet chilli sauce, but they also taste great with garlic-yogurt sauce or tahini-mayo dip.

 Serves 4   **Prep time** 10 mins   **Cook time** 15 mins   **Total time** 25 mins

2 x 400g (14oz) cans chickpeas, drained and rinsed

60g (½ cup) plain (all-purpose) flour

½ teaspoon salt

½ teaspoon ground black pepper

1 teaspoon ground cumin

1 teaspoon paprika

2 garlic cloves, peeled and minced

zest of 1 lemon

75g (¾ cup) grated (shredded) Parmesan cheese

3 tablespoons finely chopped fresh flat-leaf parsley

1 egg

4 tablespoons olive oil

To serve

sweet chilli sauce

crispy salad and/or coleslaw

1   Preheat the oven to a very low setting to keep the fritters warm (they will need to be cooked in batches). Have a baking tray ready for the fritters.

2   Place the drained chickpeas in a bowl and mash with a potato masher until the chickpeas are well broken down (it's fine if the mixture is a little lumpy). Alternatively, you can blitz in a food processor a few times until the chickpeas are broken down.

3   Add the flour, salt, pepper, cumin, paprika, garlic, lemon zest, Parmesan, parsley and egg and mix together using a fork or your hands until combined. Form into 12 patties.

4   Heat 2 tablespoons of the oil in a large frying pan (skillet) over a medium–high heat. Add six of the patties and fry for 5–6 minutes, turning once, until golden brown.

5   Remove from the pan, place on the baking tray and put in the oven to keep warm.

6   Add the remaining oil to the pan and fry the rest of the patties in the same way.

7   Once cooked, serve three patties per person, drizzled with sweet chilli sauce. I like to serve mine alongside a crispy salad or with crunchy coleslaw.

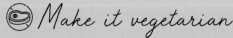

Nicky's pro tips

These fritters make great burgers! Simply halve all the quantities and make into four patties instead. Fry for an extra minute. Serve in toasted buns with lettuce, red onion and sweet chilli sauce.

Make it vegetarian

Swap the Parmesan for a vegetarian Italian-style hard cheese.

Red lentil dahl

Red lentils cook fast, without the need to soak them first, so they make a great base for a quick dahl. This creamy, lightly spicy dahl is quite saucy – perfect for scooping up with torn chapati.

Serves	Prep time	Cook time	Total time
4	10 mins	20 mins	30 mins

1 tablespoon oil or ghee
1 onion, peeled and finely diced
1 red (bell) pepper, deseeded and finely diced
3 garlic cloves, peeled and minced
1 tablespoon ginger paste
1 tablespoon garam masala
1 teaspoon ground turmeric
½ teaspoon paprika
½ teaspoon chilli (red pepper) flakes
¼ teaspoon ground fenugreek
300g (1½ cups) red lentils, rinsed
720ml (3 cups) vegetable stock
200ml (¾ cup + 1 tablespoon) canned full-fat coconut milk
¼ teaspoon salt
¼ teaspoon ground black pepper
2 tablespoons lime juice (juice from about 1 lime)
2 tablespoons salted butter

To serve
natural yogurt
chopped fresh coriander (cilantro)
chilli (red pepper) flakes
flatbreads such as chapati or naan

1 Heat the oil or ghee in a medium saucepan over a medium heat. Add the onion and red pepper and cook for 3 minutes until slightly softened.

2 Add the garlic, ginger, garam masala, turmeric, paprika, chilli flakes and fenugreek and stir together to coat the onion and pepper in the spices. Cook for 1 minute.

3 Add the lentils, stock, coconut milk, salt and pepper. Stir and bring to the boil, then simmer for 15 minutes, stirring often, until the lentils are soft and tender. Add a splash of water or stock if it starts to look too dry.

4 Turn off the heat, stir in the lime juice and butter. Swirl in a little natural yogurt, then serve topped with fresh coriander and chilli flakes.

Nicky's pro tips

This dahl freezes well. Simply cool, then freeze in portions in sealed containers. Defrost in the refrigerator overnight, then reheat in a pan, or microwave, until piping hot.

Herby lentil bowls with feta & pomegranate

This is a beautifully fragrant tabbouleh-style salad that uses green lentils instead of bulgur wheat. There's no cooking involved – more of a gathering of ingredients, so it's really quick to put together. It contains lots of fresh herbs, which act almost like salad leaves, but give the dish extra freshness. My secret ingredient – miso paste – gives this dish a lovely extra umami hit.

 Serves 4   **Prep time** 10 mins   **Cook time** 0 mins   **Total time** 10 mins

500g (1lb 2oz) ready-cooked green or Puy lentils (I like the ones in sachets that you can use without rinsing)

1 x 400g (14oz) can chickpeas, drained and rinsed

200g (7oz) cherry tomatoes, quartered

1 small red onion, peeled and finely diced

100g (3½oz) bunch of fresh coriander (cilantro), chopped

50g (1¾oz) bunch of fresh mint, chopped

100g (3½oz) bunch of fresh flat-leaf parsley, chopped

seeds from 1 pomegranate or approx. 250g (9oz) ready-prepared seeds

200g (7oz) feta

Dressing

2 tablespoons fresh lemon juice

3 tablespoons olive oil

1 tablespoon miso paste

1 tablespoon honey

¼ teaspoon ground black pepper

1 Put the cooked lentils in a large serving bowl and add the chickpeas, tomatoes, onion, coriander, parsley, mint, pomegranate and feta. Toss together to combine.

2 Mix together the dressing ingredients in a small jug or bowl. Pour over the lentil salad and toss together, then serve.

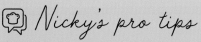 **Nicky's pro tips**

If you want to cook the lentils yourself, use 200g (7oz) dried green or Puy lentils. Rinse, then add to a pan with 1 litre (about 4 cups) cold water. Bring to the boil and simmer gently for 30–40 minutes until tender. Drain and rinse in cold water before using.

Rice, Noodles, Grains & Pulses

Spicy bean tacos with feta

At three apiece, these tacos make a filling and comforting vegetarian dinner. Marinated onions add a lip-smackingly tasty tang and the watercress adds sweetness and crunch. Add more sriracha to the beans if you like them spicy!

 Serves 4   Prep time 15 mins   Cook time 15 mins   Total time 30 mins

1 x 400g (14oz) can cannellini beans, drained and rinsed
1 x 400g (14oz) can kidney beans, drained and rinsed
300ml (1¼ cups) passata
1 teaspoon smoked paprika
½ teaspoon garlic powder
¼ teaspoon salt
⅛ teaspoon white pepper
1 tablespoon sugar
1 tablespoon sriracha

Quick marinated onions
1 red onion, peeled and thinly sliced
¼ teaspoon salt
2 tablespoons red wine vinegar
6 tablespoons olive oil
1 teaspoon dried oregano

To serve
12 soft tacos (or small wheat tortillas), warmed
1 avocado, stoned and diced
200g (7oz) feta, crumbled
30g (1 packed cup) watercress

1 Start with the marinated onions. Add the sliced onion to a small bowl. Sprinkle over the salt and pour over the red wine vinegar. Set aside for 15 minutes, giving it a stir a couple of times.

2 Add the cannellini and kidney beans to a saucepan, along with the passata, paprika, garlic, salt, pepper, sugar and sriracha. Stir together and cook over a medium heat for 10–12 minutes, stirring often and giving the beans a gentle squash with a fork a few times. Turn off the heat.

3 Now come back to the onions. Add the olive oil and oregano and stir together.

4 To assemble the tacos, place the warmed tacos on plates. Spoon the bean mixture in the middle. Sprinkle on the diced avocado and crumbled feta. Use a fork to remove the onion slices from the marinade and add them to the tacos. Top the tacos with the watercress. Serve immediately. You can also drizzle on a little of the marinade if you like.

🗨 Nicky's pro tips
Because we're making this quickly, I add the salt and vinegar to the onions first (so that the tangy flavour develops fast), then add the oil and oregano right before serving. If you're marinating the onions ahead, you can add all of the ingredients at once. They'll need about 3–4 hours to develop the flavour, but will last for 2–3 days, covered, at room temperature.

Quick & Easy

Honey garlic prawn rice bowls

£££

Make sure you get everything ready before you start cooking the prawns in this recipe, as they're done in 5 minutes! I like to keep this bowl recipe nice and simple – using microwave rice for the base and a mixture of raw chopped vegetables on top. Drizzle the sauce from the pan over the top for the perfect dressing.

 Serves 4   Prep time 10 mins   Cook time 5 mins   Total time 15 mins

2 x 250g (9oz) packets microwave basmati or long-grain rice
1 teaspoon oil
1 teaspoon unsalted butter
300g (10½oz) raw king prawns (jumbo shrimp), peeled and deveined
¼ teaspoon salt
¼ teaspoon ground black pepper
½ teaspoon paprika
2 garlic cloves, peeled and minced
3 tablespoon light soy sauce
4 tablespoons honey
½ cucumber, thinly sliced
1 avocado, stoned and chopped into chunks
½ small red onion, peeled and finely diced

To serve
1 tablespoon mixed black and white sesame seeds
3 tablespoons chopped fresh coriander (cilantro)

1   Heat the microwave rice as per the packet instructions. Once cooked, it can be left in the packets for a few minutes, while you cook the prawns.

2   Heat the oil and butter in a frying pan (skillet) over a high heat until the butter starts to bubble.

3   Season the prawns with the salt, pepper and paprika, then add to the pan and fry, turning often with a spatula, for 1–2 minutes until the prawns start to turn pink.

4   Reduce the heat to medium and add the garlic. Stir together for a further minute, then add the soy sauce and honey. Stir together for a further minute, then turn off the heat.

5   Divide the rice between bowls. Arrange the honey garlic prawns on top, along with the cucumber, avocado and red onion. Drizzle any sauce left in the pan over the prawns and rice.

6   Sprinkle on the sesame seeds and fresh coriander and serve.

Nicky's pro tips

Swap out the plain microwave rice for a flavoured one. Lime and coriander or roasted garlic flavours are firm favourites in our house.

Rice, Noodles, Grains & Pulses

153

Easy chicken lo mein

An easy chicken stir-fry, ready in about 25 minutes. The longest amount of time spent on this recipe is chopping the carrots into matchsticks, so if you have one of those fancy julienne peelers, this recipe is even faster to prepare!

 Serves 4   Prep time 10 mins   Cook time 15 mins   Total time 25 mins

200g (7oz) dried fine egg noodles
3 tablespoons oil
3 chicken breasts (about 525g/1lb 3oz), chopped into bite-size chunks
1 onion, peeled and sliced
2 garlic cloves, peeled and minced
1 large carrot, peeled and sliced into matchsticks
1 red (bell) pepper, deseeded and sliced
20 sugar snap peas (snow peas)
10 spring onions (scallions), cut into 5cm (2in) lengths
4 tablespoons oyster sauce
2 tablespoons soy sauce
2 tablespoons kecap manis (sweet soy sauce)
¼ teaspoon white pepper

To serve
2 spring onions (scallions), chopped
1 teaspoon sesame seeds
¼ teaspoon chilli (red pepper) flakes

1 Cook the noodles in a large pan of boiling water for 3–4 minutes until just cooked through. Drain and rinse in cold water to prevent them sticking together and set aside.

2 Meanwhile, heat the oil in a wok. Add the chicken and stir-fry for 5–6 minutes until cooked through.

3 Add the sliced onion and cook for a further 2 minutes to slightly soften.

4 Add the garlic, carrot, red pepper, sugar snap peas and spring onions. Stir-fry for 1 minute.

5 Add the noodles, oyster sauce, soy sauce, kecap manis and white pepper. Stir-fry over a high heat, tossing everything together, for 3–4 minutes until warmed through.

6 Serve topped with chopped spring onions, sesame seeds and chilli flakes.

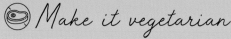

Nicky's pro tips

I like to use fine egg noodles for this recipe, but you can use medium egg noodles, wholewheat noodles or rice noodles. Even cooked spaghetti and tagliatelle works well (it sounds strange to use pasta in a Chinese recipe, but it absorbs the flavours really well). You can also use ready-cooked noodles, but you may need to run them under some hot water first to separate them.

Make it vegetarian

Leave out the chicken, or replace with tofu, mushrooms or Quorn® pieces. Replace the oyster sauce with vegetarian-style oyster or mushroom stir-fry sauce.

Baked ham & pea risotto

££

Let the oven do all the work with this easy baked risotto. You can, if you prefer, add all of the risotto ingredients to the pan at the beginning, but I find adding the peas towards the end ensures they're more vibrant and sweeter. Stirring through the Parmesan at the end makes the risotto just that little bit creamier.

 Serves 4   **Prep time** 5 mins   **Cook time** 20 mins   **Total time** 25 mins

300g (10½oz) arborio rice

1 tablespoon olive oil

½ teaspoon ground black pepper

½ teaspoon garlic powder or 2 garlic cloves, peeled and minced

¼ teaspoon celery salt

150g (1 cup) cooked ham chunks (or shredded ham hock)

700ml (3 cups) just-boiled strong chicken stock

115g (⅔ cup) frozen peas

50g (½ cup) grated (shredded) Parmesan

juice of ½ lemon

To serve

grated Parmesan

ground black pepper

chopped fresh flat-leaf parsley

1 Preheat the oven to 200°C fan/425°F/gas mark 7. Place a lidded casserole dish in the oven to heat up.

2 Once the casserole dish is hot, remove from the oven and remove the lid (leave a tea towel (dish towel) on the lid so you don't accidentally pick up the hot lid).

3 Carefully add the rice to the dish, along with the oil, pepper, garlic, celery salt, ham and hot stock. Stir together, place the lid on the pan and put in the oven for 17 minutes.

4 Remove from the oven, add the peas, Parmesan and lemon juice and stir together. Place the lid back on and return to the oven for a further 3 minutes until the rice is tender.

5 Remove from the oven and give it a taste. Add a little more salt and pepper if needed (the level of saltiness depends on how salty your ham and stock are).

6 Serve the risotto topped with extra Parmesan, black pepper and fresh parsley.

Nicky's pro tips

Swap out the ham for chunks of cooked chicken and chunky mushroom slices if you want to change this dish up.

Rice, Noodles, Grains & Pulses

Ham & pineapple fried rice

That classic pizza combination but made into fried rice instead. Personally, I think pineapple works far better in fried rice anyway! If you want to make a quick sweet and sour sauce to drizzle over the top, you can also use up the pineapple juice from the can. Simply mix 1 part pineapple juice with 1 part malt vinegar, 2 parts brown sugar and 3 parts tomato ketchup. Stir and heat in a pan for a couple of minutes until bubbling.

 Serves 4   **Prep time** 10 mins   **Cook time** 20 mins   **Total time** 30 mins

1 tablespoon rapeseed (canola) or sunflower oil

1 tablespoon sesame oil

1 onion, peeled and finely diced

1 red (bell) pepper, deseeded and diced

10 button mushrooms, sliced in half

115g (⅔ cup) frozen peas

150g (1 cup) cooked ham chunks (or shredded ham)

1 x 400g (14oz) can pineapple chunks in juice, drained

¼ teaspoon salt

¼ teaspoon ground black pepper

600g (4 cups) cooked white long-grain rice, cooled

2 tablespoons dark soy sauce

½ teaspoon garlic powder

2 eggs

juice of ½ lemon

To serve

2 spring onions (scallions), chopped

sriracha or sweet chilli sauce

lemon wedges

1   Add the rapeseed and the sesame oils to a wok over a medium–high heat. Add the onion and cook, stirring regularly, for 5 minutes until the onion softens.

2   Add the red pepper, mushrooms, peas, ham, pineapple, salt and pepper. Cook for a further 3 minutes, stirring regularly.

3   Add the cooked rice and increase the heat to high. Toss everything together using a spatula.

4   Add the soy sauce and garlic and continue to cook, moving everything around the pan regularly so it doesn't stick, until the rice is hot (this should take 5–6 minutes).

5   Once the rice is hot, push the rice over to the side of the pan and crack the eggs into the space. Move the pan so that the eggs are right over the heat. Move the eggs round slowly until they start to scramble. As they scramble, mix the eggs into the rice.

6   Add the lemon juice, stir and taste. Add more soy sauce or lemon juice if needed.

7   Divide between bowls and top with chopped spring onions, a drizzle of sriracha and some lemon wedges.

Nicky's pro tips

Make sure the boiled rice is cooled before using. This will help stop it sticking together and will ensure it absorbs more flavour. You can use ready-cooked rice if you're short on time.

Make it vegetarian

Swap out the ham for a vegetarian alternative, such as seitan.

Minced beef fajita bowls

Using minced (ground) beef instead of steak or chicken is a great way to make this fajita bowl recipe more cost-effective. You can be flexible on the toppings too – using whatever leftovers work. Chopped courgette (zucchini), peas, green beans, mushrooms and celery make great additions to the minced beef. Crunchy lettuce, white onion, cucumber, carrot sticks, tomatoes, pickled jalapeños and gherkins make great raw toppings. I change it up for whatever I have in the refrigerator at the time.

 Serves 4

 Prep time 10 mins

 Cook time 20 mins

 Total time 30 mins

200g (1 cup) long-grain rice
1 tablespoon oil
500g (1lb 2oz) minced (ground) beef
¼ teaspoon salt
¼ teaspoon ground black pepper
½ teaspoon chilli (red pepper) flakes
2 tablespoons fajita seasoning
1 red (bell) pepper, deseeded and sliced
1 yellow (bell) pepper, deseeded and sliced
2 garlic cloves, peeled and minced
1 avocado, stoned and diced
1 small red onion, peeled and thinly sliced
4 tablespoons tomato salsa
4 tablespoons sour cream
50g (½ cup) grated (shredded) Cheddar
1 lime, sliced into half-moons
chopped coriander (cilantro)
2 tablespoons sriracha or sweet chilli sauce

1. Pour 360ml (1½ cups) water into a saucepan and bring to the boil. Add the rice, stir once and place a lid on the pan. Reduce the heat to its lowest setting and cook for 20 minutes.

2. Meanwhile, add the oil to a frying pan (skillet) over a high heat. Add the beef, salt, pepper, chilli flakes and fajita seasoning. Fry for 4–5 minutes, stirring and breaking up any large clumps of mince, until the beef is light brown.

3. Add the sliced peppers and garlic and cook for a further 5 minutes, stirring often. Turn off the heat.

4. When the rice is cooked, remove the lid and divide between bowls.

5. Top with the cooked beef and peppers. Arrange the avocado, onion slices, salsa, sour cream, Cheddar and lime slices in the bowls. Sprinkle on the coriander and drizzle on the chilli sauce, then serve.

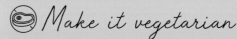 *Nicky's pro tips*

I use beef with 20% fat in this recipe for more juiciness and flavour. You can use a lower-fat version, but it will be a little drier once fried. You can add a little drizzle of oil and a splash of beef stock if you wish to add more moisture.

Make it vegetarian

Swap the beef for vegetarian mince or very finely diced mushrooms.

Rice, Noodles, Grains & Pulses

Peanut butter ramen with beef

££

Most of the time for this quick ramen is spent boiling the eggs, so if you boil them ahead of time, this meal can be ready in as little as 15 minutes! We're using speedy shortcuts of ramen noodle packets and cooked, sliced deli/sandwich beef to make this a flavourful dinner you can have on the table in no time.

 Serves 4

 Prep time 15 mins

 Cook time 15 mins

 Total time 30 mins

4 eggs, at room temperature
1 tablespoon sesame oil
2 tablespoons unsalted butter
4 garlic cloves, peeled and minced
2 teaspoons minced ginger
1.4 litres (about 6 cups) beef stock (water plus 4 beef stock cubes is fine)
2 tablespoons smooth peanut butter
2 tablespoons light soy sauce
1–2 tablespoons sriracha sauce
1 tablespoon Chinese rice wine or sherry
1 tablespoon light brown sugar
¼ teaspoon white pepper
3 x 70g (2½oz) packets instant noodles (noodles only)
100g (3½oz) packet cooked peppered beef slices, sliced into thin strips

Toppings
5 spring onions (scallions), chopped
1 carrot, peeled and sliced thinly
1 teaspoon black and white sesame seeds
a pinch of chilli (red pepper) flakes

1 Start by boiling the eggs. Place them in a medium saucepan and cover with cold water. Bring to the boil, then simmer for 6 minutes. After 6 minutes, place the eggs in a bowl of water with ice and allow to cool for 5 minutes.

2 Peel the eggs (to make things easier, I roll them on the work surface to break the shell all over), then slice in half.

3 Now make the ramen. Heat the oil and butter in a large saucepan over a medium heat until the butter melts. Add the garlic and ginger and fry for 30 seconds, stirring constantly.

4 Add the stock, peanut butter, soy sauce, sriracha, rice wine, sugar and pepper. Stir together and bring to the boil.

5 Add the instant noodles, bring back to the boil, then simmer for 3 minutes, stirring occasionally, to separate the noodles.

6 Add the strips of beef and cook for 30 seconds to heat through.

7 Use a set of tongs to divide the noodles between bowls. Ladle over the sauce and beef. Top each bowl with two halves of egg. Garnish the ramen with the spring onions, carrot, sesame seeds and chilli flakes.

Nicky's pro tips
You can make the eggs a day or two ahead of time. Boil the eggs, then cool and remove the shells. Place in a sealed container, in the refrigerator, and slice in half just before serving.

Make it vegetarian
Replace the beef stock with vegetable stock and replace the sliced beef with your favourite vegetarian sandwich-slice alternative (vegetarian-style smoky ham or chicken slices work well).

Teriyaki minced beef noodles

££

I like to make up a double or triple batch of this teriyaki sauce when I'm cooking this minced beef noodle dish. It can be stored in the refrigerator, where it easily lasts a week or two. It makes a great standby stir-fry sauce and marinade for chicken and steak, or for a quick veggie stir-fry.

 Serves 4   Prep time 10 mins   Cook time 15 mins   Total time 25 mins

1 tablespoon sesame oil
500g (1lb 2oz) minced (ground) beef (12–20% fat is best for more flavour)
½ teaspoon salt
½ teaspoon ground black pepper
150g (1 cup) mangetout, sliced on the diagonal
1 red (bell) pepper, deseeded and thinly sliced
5 spring onions (scallions), sliced on the diagonal, plus a couple extra, sliced, to serve
400g (14oz) fresh (cooked) egg noodles (see Tip)

Teriyaki sauce
2 tablespoons light soy sauce
3 tablespoons dark soy sauce
1 tablespoon sake or dry sherry
3 tablespoons mirin
1 teaspoon sesame oil
1 tablespoon brown sugar
2 teaspoons minced ginger
3 garlic cloves, peeled and minced
½ teaspoon white pepper
1 tablespoon cornflour (cornstarch)

To serve
1 tablespoon mixed black and white sesame seeds
1 red chilli, finely sliced

1. First make the sauce. Mix all the ingredients in a bowl until the cornflour is fully incorporated. Set aside.

2. Heat the sesame oil in a wok over a high heat.

3. Add the beef, salt and pepper and stir-fry for 5 minutes until browned. Stir regularly with a spatula, breaking up any large clumps of beef as you go.

4. Add the mangetout, red pepper and spring onions and stir-fry for a further 5 minutes, so they're warm but still have some crunch.

5. Add the fresh noodles along with the teriyaki sauce. Stir-fry for a final 5 minutes, tossing everything together with the spatula until the noodles are warmed through and the sauce coats everything.

6. Divide between bowls and top with the sesame seeds, red chilli and spring onions, then serve.

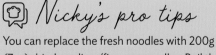 *Nicky's pro tips*

You can replace the fresh noodles with 200g (7oz) dried medium/fine egg noodles. Boil them in water as per the packet instructions (usually 3–5 minutes), then drain and run under cold water, to stop the cooking process. Toss with 1 tablespoon of sesame oil to stop them sticking together. Then use in the same way as the fresh noodles.

Rice, Noodles, Grains & Pulses

Beef chow mein

Tender steak strips with chow mein noodles and vegetables in a tasty stir-fry sauce. I love this beef chow mein for a quick dinner that everyone enjoys. It's not spicy, just full of umami flavour.

 Serves 4   **Prep time** 15 mins   **Cook time** 15 mins   **Total time** 30 mins

150g (5½oz) dried chow mein or fine egg noodles
3 tablespoons oil
300g (10½oz) thin sirloin, skirt or flank steak, sliced thinly, against the grain
¼ teaspoon garlic salt
½ teaspoon ground black pepper
1 small onion, peeled and sliced
2 garlic cloves, peeled and minced
1 carrot, peeled and sliced into matchsticks
½ green (bell) pepper, deseeded and sliced
¼ Savoy cabbage, thinly sliced
100 g (3½oz) bean sprouts

Chow mein sauce
1 tablespoon cornflour (cornstarch)
2 tablespoons dark soy sauce
1 tablespoon Chinese rice wine
2 tablespoons kecap manis
2 tablespoons hoisin sauce
90ml (⅓ cup) beef stock
1 tablespoon sesame oil
¼ teaspoon white pepper

To serve
chopped spring onions (scallions)
sesame seeds
chilli (red pepper) flakes

1. Cook the noodles in boiling water, as per the packet instructions. Drain and run under cold water to stop them sticking together. Set aside.

2. While the noodles are cooking, make the chow mein sauce. In a small bowl, mix together the cornflour, soy sauce and Chinese rice wine until the cornflour is fully incorporated. Then add in the kecap manis, hoisin sauce, beef stock, sesame oil and white pepper. Mix together to combine and set aside.

3. Heat 2 tablespoons of the oil in a wok over a high heat. Season the steak strips in the garlic salt and pepper, then add to the wok and fry for 2–3 minutes, turning once or twice, until the steak is just cooked. Remove the steak from the pan with a slotted spoon and place in a bowl.

4. Add the remaining tablespoon of oil to the wok. Add the onion, garlic and carrot and stir-fry for 3 minutes, regularly tossing everything together with a spatula.

5. Add the green pepper, cabbage and bean sprouts and stir-fry for a further 2 minutes, keeping everything moving in the wok with your spatula.

6. Now add the steak strips back to the wok, along with the noodles. Pour the chow mein sauce over the top. Stir-fry everything together for 2–3 minutes, tossing regularly with a set of tongs, until the noodles are hot.

7. Serve topped with spring onions, sesame seeds and chilli flakes.

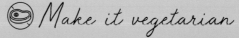

Nicky's pro tips

Place the steak in the freezer for 30–40 minutes before slicing. This will make the meat firmer and easier to slice thinly.

Make it vegetarian

Swap out the steak for chunky mushrooms pieces. Replace the beef stock with vegetable stock.

Snack
Suppers

Dinner doesn't always have to be a full-on dining-table experience.

· Sometimes we want a quick, lighter meal.
· Sometimes we want breakfast for dinner.
· Sometimes we want to use a garlic baguette to make a sandwich.

Oh, is that just me? Yes, that would be my **Buffalo chicken-stuffed garlic bread** (see page 178) that my kids went so wild over that you'd think they'd just won the lottery!

Have you ever tried **Savoury pancakes**? My fluffy pancakes are stuffed with shredded ham hock, peas and sweetcorn and finished with a moreish **salted honey butter topping** (see page 185).

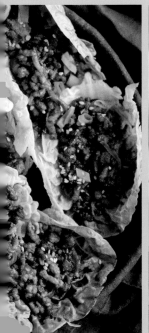

Creamy garlic & mushroom stuffed breads

These stuffed rolls have delicious, creamy garlic cheesiness stuffed into petits pains and baked until golden brown. Super easy to make and ready in 15 minutes! They work great as a snack dinner, luscious lunch or interesting appetizer.

 Serves
4

 Prep time
5 mins

 Cook time
10 mins

 Total time
15 mins

4 part-baked petits pains or rolls
8 small mushrooms, sliced
120g (½ cup) cream cheese
3 tablespoons crème fraîche
1 garlic clove, peeled and minced
75g (¾ cup firmly packed) grated (shredded) mature (sharp) Cheddar
a pinch of ground black pepper
2 tablespoons chopped fresh parsley, to serve

1   Preheat the oven to 200°C fan/425°F/gas mark 7.

2   Take the part-baked rolls out of the packaging and place on a chopping board. Using a sharp knife, carefully cut out an oblong hole from the top of the rolls. Scoop out the bread, ensuring you don't pierce the bottom of the rolls.

3   Place the rolls on a baking tray. Discard the scooped-out bread (or save to use for homemade breadcrumbs or croutons).

4   Mix together the mushrooms, cream cheese, crème fraîche and garlic in a bowl. Stir in 50g (½ cup firmly packed) of the cheese and the black pepper. Spoon the mixture into the bread rolls. Top the stuffed bread rolls with the remaining 25g (¼ cup firmly packed) cheese.

5   Bake in the oven for 10 minutes until the bread and cheese are golden brown.

6   Remove from the oven and sprinkle with fresh parsley before serving.

Nicky's pro tips

You can make the filling ahead of time or make the filling and stuff the breads (but don't bake). Make up to a day ahead, then store, covered, in the refrigerator until ready to bake.

Cinnamon sugar French toast

£

Who says you can't have breakfast for dinner?! Sometimes we make a proper breakfast fry-up for dinner. Occasionally it's a bowl of cereal (I think it tastes better at night than in the morning). But every now and then, I want something simple and sweet for dinner. This cinnamon-sugar encrusted French toast totally hits the spot. Serve it on its own, with fruit, or pile it high with whipped cream and chopped nuts!

 Serves 2   **Prep time** 5 mins   **Cook time** 10 mins   **Total time** 15 mins

2 large eggs
4 tablespoons full-fat (whole) milk
½ teaspoon vanilla extract
6 tablespoons soft light brown sugar
2 teaspoons ground cinnamon
4 tablespoons unsalted butter
6 thick slices of brioche bread

Serving suggestions
icing (confectioners') sugar, for dusting
fresh berries, cherries, or banana slices
golden or maple syrup
whipped cream
chopped nuts, such as hazelnuts, pecans, or walnuts

1. Whisk together the eggs, milk and vanilla extract in a wide, shallow bowl.

2. Place the sugar and cinnamon on a plate and mix.

3. Heat half the butter in a large frying pan (skillet) over a medium heat until just bubbling.

4. Dip three of the bread slices in the egg mixture and turn so that both sides are covered. Place the bread straight in the hot pan. Fry for 1–2 minutes on each side until light brown.

5. While the toast is still in the pan, sprinkle over 1 tablespoon of the cinnamon sugar, turn the toast over and sprinkle with another tablespoon of cinnamon sugar. Cook for a further minute on each side until golden brown.

6. Transfer to a warm plate and add the remaining butter to the pan. Repeat with the remaining bread slices.

7. Once all the French toast slices are cooked, divide between plates and serve with an extra sprinkling of the remaining cinnamon sugar.

8. Serve as it is, or top with extra toppings (see serving suggestions). As an extra treat, I like to serve this with raspberries, whipped cream, chopped nuts and a drizzle of maple syrup.

Nicky's pro tips
Prefer French toast fingers? Slice the bread into fingers before dipping in the egg mixture. You may need a little more cinnamon sugar to coat all the sides!

Snack Suppers

173

Avocado & feta egg bagels

I've just discovered that egg cooked into the middle of toasted bread is called 'toad in the hole' in the USA. Very different from the UK version! The trick to getting the white to set and the yolk to stay runny is to use a frying pan (skillet) with a lid. This keeps the heat circulating around the egg, so the white cooks from the top and the bottom.

 Serves 2   **Prep time** 10 mins   **Cook time** 5 mins   **Total time** 15 mins

2 bagels
2 tablespoons salted butter
2 small eggs
4 tablespoons crumbled feta
2 tablespoons chopped fresh coriander (cilantro)
1 tablespoon sweet chilli sauce
a pinch of salt and pepper

Avocado filling
1 ripe avocado
1 teaspoon fresh lime juice
⅛ teaspoon salt
⅛ teaspoon ground black pepper

1   Slice the bagels in half horizontally. Make the hole in the top half of the bagels bigger using a knife. It needs to be about 2cm (¾in) in diameter. Spread the cut sides of the bagels with the butter.

2. Heat a large frying pan (skillet) over a low–medium heat and place the bagels in the pan, cut-side-down.

3. Break an egg into a small bowl then carefully pour it into the hole of the top half of one of the bagels (don't worry if it runs out a little). Repeat with the other egg, so both bagel tops have an egg in them. Sprinkle a pinch of salt and pepper on the eggs.

4. Place a lid on the pan (or use foil) and cook for 3–4 minutes, checking a few times, until the egg white is cooked and the yolk is still soft. If you find the bottom halves of the bagels are browning more than you'd like, you can take them out of the pan (the top halves will be protected as some of the egg white will have run underneath them).

5. Meanwhile, slice open the avocado, remove the stone and scoop the flesh into a small bowl. Add the lime juice, salt and pepper and mash the avocado with a fork.

6. Place the bases of the bagels on plates and spoon on the avocado mixture. Sprinkle on the crumbled feta, chopped coriander and drizzle with sweet chilli sauce.

7. Using a spatula, carefully remove the egg-bagel-tops and place on top of the avocado mixture. Serve immediately.

Nicky's pro tips
Speed up this snack supper even more by using store-bought guacamole.

Chicken quesadillas

££

There's something about the cheesy gooiness of quesadillas that makes them so addictive and a real treat dinner! The kids love them as a snack dinner if we want something quick and not too filling, but if I want to serve these as part of bigger meal I add spicy rice or chips and a big crunchy salad.

 Serves 4   **Prep time** 10 mins   **Cook time** 20 mins   **Total time** 30 mins

3 tablespoons oil
4 chicken thigh fillets, chopped into small chunks
¼ teaspoon salt
¼ teaspoon ground black pepper
1 tablespoon taco seasoning
1 small onion, peeled and thinly sliced
1 red (bell) pepper, deseeded and chopped into small chunks
4 medium mushrooms, sliced
4 large flour tortillas
200g (2 packed cups) grated (shredded) mixed cheese (I use a mixture of Cheddar and red Leicester)
4 spring onions (scallions), sliced

To serve
lime wedges
chopped fresh coriander (cilantro)
sour cream

1   Preheat the oven to very low and put a baking tray to one side (this is for keeping the quesadillas warm).

2   Heat 2 tablespoons of the oil in a large frying pan (skillet) over a medium–high heat.

3   Add the chicken, salt, pepper, taco seasoning, onion, red pepper and mushrooms. Cook for 8–9 minutes, stirring often, until the chicken is cooked through. Remove from the pan and place in a bowl.

4   Place a tortilla on a board and sprinkle a quarter of the cheese on one half of the tortilla. Spoon a quarter of the chicken mixture on top of the cheese, followed by a quarter of the chopped spring onions. Fold the tortilla in half and repeat with the remaining three tortillas.

5   Wipe the pan clean and place over a medium heat. Add ½ tablespoon of oil. Place two of the folded tortillas in the pan. Cook for 2–3 minutes on each side until the tortillas are golden and the cheese has melted.

6   Remove from the pan and repeat with the remaining two tortillas. You can place the cooked quesadillas on a tray in the warm oven until the second batch is ready.

7   Once they are all cooked, transfer to a chopping board and slice in half.

8   Serve with lime wedges, chopped coriander and sour cream for dipping.

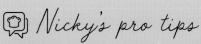 Nicky's pro tips
Use ready-cooked/leftover shredded chicken if you prefer. This will cut down the time for frying the chicken and vegetables to 5–6 minutes.

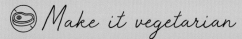 Make it vegetarian
Replace the chicken with extra vegetables, tofu or Quorn® pieces.

Snack Suppers

Buffalo chicken-stuffed garlic bread

I've usually got a garlic baguette somewhere at the back of the freezer,
so this makes a great, filling dinner when you fancy a gourmet sandwich.

 Serves 4 **Prep time** 10 mins **Cook time** 20 mins **Total time** 30 mins

2 fresh or frozen store-bought garlic baguettes (about 200g/7oz each)

2 tablespoons oil

2 chicken breasts (about 350g/12oz), chopped into bite-size pieces

1 tablespoon Cajun spice mix

½ teaspoon ground black pepper

1 chicken stock (bouillon) cube, crumbled

1 onion, peeled and sliced

1 red (bell) pepper, deseeded and sliced

1 yellow (bell) pepper, deseeded and sliced

2 garlic cloves, peeled and minced

2 jalapeños (or medium heat green chillies), sliced

60ml (¼ cup) hot pepper sauce

1 tablespoon Worcestershire sauce

1 tablespoon cider vinegar

100ml (⅓ cup + 1 tablespoon) double (heavy) cream

50g (½ cup) grated (shredded) Cheddar

3 spring onions (scallions), roughly chopped

1. Preheat the oven to 180°C fan/400°F/gas mark 6 (or the temperature stated on the garlic baguette packet).

2. If using fresh baguettes, carefully slice halfway through both breads, down the middle, lengthways. This will allow you to stuff them later. If using frozen, wait until they're cooked to do this.

3. Place the baguettes on a baking tray and cook as per the packet instructions. Meanwhile, make the buffalo chicken. Heat the oil in a large frying pan (skillet) over a medium–high heat. Add the chicken to the pan and sprinkle over the Cajun spice mix and black pepper. Stir to coat the chicken and cook for 5 minutes, stirring occasionally, until the chicken is sealed and nearly cooked through.

4. Sprinkle over the stock cube and stir together. Add the onion, red and yellow peppers, garlic and half the jalapeños. Stir together and cook for 5 minutes, stirring often, until the onion softens slightly.

5. Add the hot sauce, Worcestershire sauce, cider vinegar and cream. Stir together and bring to a simmer. Simmer for 4–5 minutes, stirring occasionally, until the chicken is fully cooked through. Turn off the heat.

6. By now the baguettes should be cooked through. While still on the tray, carefully open up the baguettes along the lengthways slice (if you used frozen baguettes, carefully slice lengthways at this point).

7. Spoon the buffalo chicken mixture into the baguettes and sprinkle over the cheese. Return to the oven for 2–3 minutes until the cheese has melted.

8. Remove from the oven, halve each baguette (half a baguette per person) and sprinkle with the remaining sliced jalapeños and the chopped spring onions before serving.

> 💬 *Nicky's pro tips*
>
> Don't like it too hot? You can swap out the Cajun spice mix for mild fajita seasoning, then halve the amount of hot pepper sauce and leave out the jalapeños. It will still have a little kick but will be much milder.

Make it vegetarian

Swap out the chicken for tofu or Quorn® and switch the Worcestershire sauce for a vegetarian Worcestershire sauce (available from most big supermarkets).

Crispy baked Parmesan chicken strips

£££

Nothing pleases my kids more than a plateful of chicken strips! Serve these on their own with your favourite sauce, pile them into wraps or burger buns, with chips, or slice and serve on a big salad with a drizzle of creamy salad dressing.

 Serves 4   Prep time 10 mins   Cook time 20 mins   Total time 30 mins

2 eggs, lightly beaten
90g (¾ cup) plain (all-purpose) flour
100g (2 cups) panko breadcrumbs
100g (1 cup) finely grated (shredded) Parmesan
1 teaspoon paprika
½ teaspoon salt
½ teaspoon ground black pepper
2 tablespoons olive oil
4 large chicken breasts (about 800g/1lb 12oz), cut into finger-width strips

Special sauce
3 tablespoons tomato ketchup
3 tablespoons mayonnaise
½ tablespoon mild yellow mustard

1   Preheat the oven to 200°C fan/425°F/gas mark 7.

2   Put the beaten egg in one bowl and the flour in a second bowl. Put the breadcrumbs, Parmesan, paprika, salt, pepper and olive oil in a third bowl and mix well (the oil should coat the breadcrumbs, but the mixture shouldn't stick together).

3   Dip the chicken strips into the flour, then coat in the egg and finally coat in the breadcrumbs. Place on two baking sheets. Try to ensure they're not too close together, otherwise they won't go crispy.

4   Bake in the oven for 15–20 minutes until golden brown.

5   While the chicken is in the oven, make the special sauce by mixing the ketchup, mayonnaise and mustard together in a small bowl. Set aside.

6   When the chicken is brown, cut one of the strips in half to ensure it's cooked through. It should be hot throughout with no trace of pink.

7   Serve the chicken strips with the special sauce.

Nicky's pro tips
If you want to fry the chicken strips instead of baking, leave the olive oil out of the breadcrumb coating. Shallow-fry the chicken strips in 1cm (½in) of oil in a large frying pan (skillet) over a medium–high heat for 8–10 minutes until golden and cooked through. You may need to work in two batches to ensure the pan isn't overcrowded.

Snack Suppers

Spicy turkey lettuce wraps

Golden fried turkey with a lovely sweet-spicy-savoury flavour, stuffed into crisp lettuce leaves and topped with all the toppings! No knife and fork required, I just serve these up on a big board or tray and everyone digs in.

Serves
4

Prep time
5 mins

Cook time
10 mins

Total time
15 mins

2 tablespoons sesame oil
500g (1lb 2oz) minced (ground) turkey
2 garlic cloves, peeled and minced
1 red chilli, thinly sliced
2 tablespoons light brown sugar
2 tablespoons hoisin sauce
1 tablespoon dark soy sauce
¼ teaspoon white pepper
2 tablespoons water

To serve
12 baby gem lettuce leaves, washed and dried
6 spring onions (scallions), finely sliced
2 teaspoons sesame seeds
½ teaspoon chilli (red pepper) flakes
sweet chilli sauce or sriracha, to taste

1   Heat the oil in a frying pan (skillet) over a high heat. Add the turkey and fry for 5 minutes, breaking up any large clumps as you go, until lightly browned.

2   Add the garlic and chilli and fry for another 2 minutes.

3   Add the sugar, hoisin and soy sauces, pepper and water and stir together. Fry for a further 2 minutes until the turkey is golden brown. Turn off the heat.

4   Divide the turkey between the baby gem leaves. Top with spring onions, sesame seeds, chilli flakes and finish with a drizzle of chilli sauce before serving.

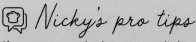 *Nicky's pro tips*

If you want to make these wraps a little more substantial, you can add some rice. Either add 1 tablespoon of freshly boiled/steamed rice to each lettuce leaf, or alternatively, add 200g (1⅓ cups) cooked rice to the pan with the cooked turkey and stir together before spooning into the lettuce leaves.

20-minute butter bean chorizo soup

Almost like a hearty, slightly spicy stew, this bean soup with chorizo is filling and super-flavourful. Topping it off with feta and watercress takes the soup to a whole new level!

Serves
2

Prep time
5 mins

Cook time
15 mins

Total time
20 mins

1 teaspoon oil
1 onion, peeled and finely diced
85g (3oz) chorizo, chopped into chunks
1 x 400g (14oz) can chopped tomatoes
300ml (1¼ cups) chicken stock
1 tablespoon tomato purée (paste)

1 teaspoon sugar
½ teaspoon dried thyme
a pinch of salt and pepper
1 x 400g (14oz) can butter (lima), beans drained and rinsed

To serve
45g (1½oz) feta, crumbled
a handful of fresh watercress roughly, torn

1   Heat the oil in a large frying pan (skillet) over a medium heat. Add the onion and chorizo and fry for 5–6 minutes until the onion starts to turn translucent and the chorizo is lightly browned and starting to release its oils.

2   Add the canned tomatoes, stock, tomato purée, sugar, thyme, salt and pepper and simmer for 7–8 minutes, stirring occasionally.

3   Add the butter beans, stir and cook for 2 minutes until warmed through.

4   Ladle into bowls and top with crumbled feta and watercress.

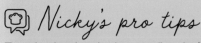

Nicky's pro tips

To make ahead, make the soup (but don't add the feta and watercress toppings until you come to serve it), cool, cover and refrigerate for 2–3 days. Reheat in a pan over a medium heat, stirring often, until piping hot (about 5 minutes). This soup can also be frozen. Simply defrost in the refrigerator overnight, then reheat as above.

Snack Suppers

Savoury pancakes with salted honey butter

Pancakes don't need to be sweet – they make a brilliant savoury option for dinner. Quick to prepare and a bit of a novelty that the kids especially enjoy! I make lots of different versions of these pancakes – using crispy bacon, cooked potato, goat's cheese, chorizo, sliced chillies, the possibilities are endless!

 Serves 4   Prep time 15 mins   Cook time 15 mins   Total time 30 mins

240g (2 cups) self-raising flour

1 teaspoon baking powder

a pinch of salt

1 large egg

360ml (1½ cups) full-fat (whole) milk

8 spring onions (scallions), finely chopped, plus extra to serve

85g (½ cup) frozen peas, defrosted

85g (½ cup) frozen or canned and drained sweetcorn (thaw if using frozen sweetcorn)

100g (½ cup) shredded cooked ham hock

1 tablespoon oil

Salted honey butter

6 tablespoons unsalted butter, softened

2 tablespoons honey

½ teaspoon sea salt

1. Preheat the oven to a very low setting to keep the pancakes warm (they will need to be cooked in batches). Put a baking tray to one side for the pancakes.

2. Put the flour, baking powder, salt and egg in a large mixing bowl. Start to mix with a balloon whisk, while slowly pouring in the milk, until you have a thick batter. Don't worry if there are a few lumps.

3. Add the spring onions, peas, sweetcorn and shredded ham and carefully fold together.

4. Heat a large frying pan (skillet) over a low-medium heat and brush on a little of the oil.

5. Add blobs of pancake batter to the pan – about 4 tablespoons (¼ cup) per pancake. I usually make three pancakes at a time. Fry for 1½–2 minutes until bubbles appear on top of the pancakes, then turn the pancakes over, using a spatula, and cook for a further 1–2 minutes until lightly browned.

6. Transfer to the baking tray and place in the oven. Continue to make pancakes, in the same way, with the remaining mixture. You should get 12 pancakes altogether.

7. While the pancakes are cooking, make the salted honey butter by mixing the butter, honey and salt together in a small bowl. Set aside.

8. When the pancakes are ready, divide between plates. Sprinkle on the remaining spring onions and top with a spoonful of salted honey butter.

Nicky's pro tips

It's easiest use a non-stick pan over a low–medium heat when making pancakes. This will ensure they're browned on the outside and cooked in the middle.

Snack Suppers

Crispy lamb salad

Crispy shreds of lamb paired with creamy feta, crunchy red onion and tangy roasted semi-dried tomatoes, all finished off with a simple balsamic dressing. This is my absolute favourite salad of all time and hands down the best way to use up those roast dinner leftovers.

 Serves 4   **Prep time** 5 mins   **Cook time** 10 mins   **Total time** 15 mins

3 tablespoons oil

300g (10½oz) leftover roast lamb, shredded

2 tablespoons cornflour (cornstarch)

¼ teaspoon salt

¼ teaspoon ground black pepper

140g (5oz) baby salad leaves

150g (5½oz) semi-dried tomatoes in olive oil, drained (you can mix the drained oil with the balsamic for your salad dressing if you like)

½ medium cucumber, sliced

½ large red onion, peeled and sliced thinly

100g (½ cup) feta, crumbled

Dressing

4 tablespoons good-quality balsamic vinegar

3 tablespoons olive oil

a large pinch of salt and pepper

1 Heat the oil in a large pan or wok (a high-sided pan is best to reduce oil spattering), over a high heat.

2 Coat the lamb in the cornflour, salt and pepper. When the oil is hot, add the lamb to the pan. Cook for 5–6 minutes, turning every minute, until the lamb is crispy and brown.

3 While the lamb is cooking, make the dressing by mixing the dressing ingredients together.

4 Arrange the salad leaves on plates or one large serving platter.

5 When the lamb is ready, remove from the pan with a slotted spoon and place on some kitchen paper to soak up any excess oil.

6 Top the salad leaves with the crispy lamb, then add the tomatoes and cucumber. Sprinkle on the red onion slices and feta. Serve, drizzled with the balsamic dressing.

💬 *Nicky's pro tips*

You can swap out the lamb for leftover cooked beef or chicken if you like.

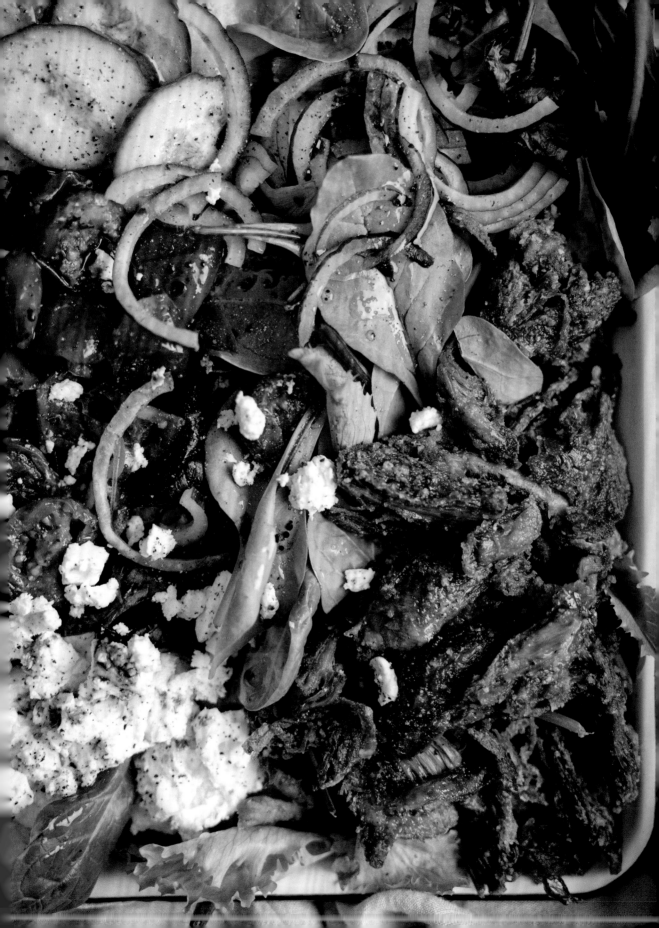

Pizza toasts

£

Cheese on toast with an upgrade! You can use homemade or store-bought pizza sauce for this recipe if you like, but I find the rest of the jar never gets used. Instead, I like to mix up a quick no-cook pizza sauce from a few store-cupboard ingredients, which works just as well to give that tomatoey tang.

 Serves 4

 Prep time 5 mins

 Cook time 10 mins

 Total time 15 mins

4 thick slices of bread (I like to use sourdough or tiger bread for a crispier crust)
1 tablespoon tomato purée (paste)
3 tablespoons tomato ketchup
1 teaspoon olive oil
½ teaspoon dried oregano
¼ teaspoon garlic powder
150g (1½ packed cups) grated (shredded) mixed cheese (I use a mixture of Cheddar, mozzarella and red Leicester)
4 cherry tomatoes, sliced
6 slices pepperoni, quartered

To serve
¼ teaspoon dried oregano
2 spring onions (scallions), sliced

1   Lightly toast the bread on both sides under the grill (broiler).

2   Mix together the tomato purée, ketchup, olive oil, oregano and garlic in a small bowl. Top the toast slices with the sauce and spread to the edges.

3   Sprinkle on the grated cheese, then arrange the tomato slices and pepperoni pieces on top. Place back under the grill on a high heat for 3–5 minutes until the cheese is melted and bubbling.

4   Serve topped with a sprinkling of dried oregano and spring onions.

Nicky's pro tips

Swap out the toppings to change up the pizza toasts. Sliced mushrooms, jalapeños, pineapple chunks, shredded ham and diced peppers all work well. You can also add a spoonful of pesto to the pizza sauce for extra flavour.

Snack Suppers

Super
Sauces

I can't tell you how many times dinner has been saved by remembering I have a prepared sauce in the refrigerator or freezer.

All of them are versatile, easily adapted and simple to prepare. They can all be frozen, so they make a great option if you want to batch-cook some sauces and have them on standby.

I've included some 'how to use' instructions with each of the sauces, so you have some ideas of the different ways they can be made into complete meals.

Tomato ragù

A flavourful ragù often needs long simmering. This recipe uses a couple of shortcuts to get that rich flavour in less time: blending the vegetables to make them cook and start to caramelize quicker (also great for people who prefer smooth sauces) and adding in extra flavour with Marmite® and Worcestershire sauce.

 Serves 4–6   **Prep time** 5 mins   **Cook time** 15 mins   **Total time** 20 mins

1 large onion, peeled and roughly chopped

1 celery stick, roughly chopped

1 red (bell) pepper, deseeded and roughly chopped

3 garlic cloves, peeled

3 tablespoons olive oil

800ml (3 ⅓ cups) passata

2 tablespoons tomato purée (paste)

1 teaspoon Marmite®

1 tablespoon Worcestershire sauce (or vegetarian equivalent)

1 tablespoon sugar

½ teaspoon salt

½ teaspoon ground black pepper

1 teaspoon dried oregano

1   Place the onion, celery, red pepper and garlic in a food processor and pulse until you have a smooth paste.

2   Heat the oil in a large frying pan (skillet) over a medium–high heat. Add the paste and cook for 5 minutes, stirring a couple of times, until the liquid at the edges has evaporated and the mixture has thickened slightly.

3   Add the passata, tomato purée, Marmite®, Worcestershire sauce, sugar, salt, pepper and oregano. Stir together and bring to the boil, then simmer for 10 minutes until slightly reduced and thickened.

HOW TO USE

- Mix with cooked spaghetti, pasta shapes or ravioli for a pasta ragù.

- Spoon over nachos and top with guacamole and grated (shredded) cheese for a simple nacho dinner.

- Pour over cooked breaded chicken and top with torn mozzarella, then grill, for homemade chicken Parmesan.

- Stir with cooked minced (ground) or shredded meat (chicken, beef or pulled pork works great) for a meaty ragù.

- Simmer for longer to thicken the sauce further and use as a pizza sauce.

- Turn it into a spicy ragù by adding 1–2 tablespoons of sriracha.

- Turn it into a creamy ragù by adding 4 tablespoons of double (heavy) cream.

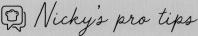 *Nicky's pro tips*

You can easily double or triple this recipe and store it in portions in the freezer. It will take a couple of minutes longer to fry the vegetable mixture and an extra 10-15 minutes of simmering if you're doubling or tripling – but it saves a lot of time on your next meal!

Lentil & red pepper sauce

This recipe started off as a soup, but by making it a little thicker, it makes a lovely, creamy sauce. It's versatile and works well with pasta, made into a mild curry (with a few tweaks), or simply as a sauce to pour over your favourite protein and vegetables.

 Serves
4

 Prep time
5 mins

 Cook time
25 mins

 Total time
30 mins

2 tablespoons olive oil

1 onion, peeled and chopped

2 red (bell) peppers, deseeded and chopped

2 garlic cloves, peeled and minced

½ teaspoon salt

½ teaspoon ground black pepper

100g (½ cup) red lentils

480ml (2 cups) vegetable stock

2 tablespoons crème fraîche

1   Heat the oil in a large saucepan over a medium heat. Add the onion, red peppers, garlic, salt and pepper and fry for 5 minutes until the onion starts to soften.

2   Add the lentils and stock. Stir together and bring to the boil. Reduce the heat and simmer for 18–20 minutes until the lentils are tender.

3   Turn off the heat and stir through the crème fraîche. If you'd like a smooth sauce, carefully blend, using a stick blender.

HOW TO USE

Vegetarian

- Stir into cooked pasta and sprinkle with grated (shredded) Cheddar for creamy lentil pasta.

- Heat with cooked tofu pieces and 1 tablespoon of curry paste and serve with rice, topped with fresh coriander (cilantro) for a mild lentil curry bowl. Add in some quick-cook vegetables, such as courgette (zucchini) or sugar snap peas (snow peas) for some extra veg too.

- Heat with an extra cup of stock (and blend together if not already blended) and serve as a soup with crusty bread.

Non-vegetarian

- Heat with cooked chicken and 1 tablespoon of curry paste and serve with rice, topped with fresh coriander (cilantro) for a mild lentil curry bowl. Add in some quick-cook vegetables – such as courgette (zucchini) or sugar snap peas (snow peas) for some extra veg too.

- Drizzle over roasted chicken thighs and serve with steamed vegetables. I like to finish with a spoonful of chilli oil or sriracha too.

Super Sauces

Pesto three ways

I love the vibrant glossy colour of fresh pesto. That tangy, rich flavour, with saltiness from the Parmesan and a lovely garlicky kick works so well to level up many recipes and to turn base ingredients into a complete meal. These three pesto recipes can also be made vegetarian by swapping out the Parmesan for vegetarian Italian-style hard cheese.

 Serves 4　　 Prep time 10 mins　　 Cook time 0 mins　　 Total time 10 mins

Basil pesto

50g (1¾oz) bunch of fresh basil, leaves only
2 garlic cloves, peeled
3 tablespoons pine nuts
30g (⅓ cup) grated (shredded) Parmesan
¼ teaspoon sea salt, plus extra to taste if needed
¼ teaspoon ground black pepper
90ml (⅓ cup) olive oil

1 Add the basil, garlic, pine nuts, Parmesan, salt and pepper to a food processor and pulse for about 10 seconds to break up the garlic and pine nuts.

2 Turn the food processor back on and pour in the oil in a steady stream, which should take about 10 seconds. Check for consistency – if you like your pesto a little chunky, it's ready to go. If you like it smoother, whizz for another 10–20 seconds until the texture is to your liking.

3 Taste the pesto and add more lightly crushed sea salt if needed.

Red pepper pesto

450g (1lb) jar roasted red peppers, drained
2 garlic cloves, peeled
3 tablespoons ground (powdered) almonds
30g (⅓ cup) grated (shredded) Parmesan
¼ teaspoon sea salt, plus extra to taste if needed
¼ teaspoon ground black pepper
2 tablespoons olive oil

1 Add the peppers, garlic, almonds, Parmesan, salt, pepper and olive oil to a food processor and pulse until combined.

2 Taste the pesto and add more salt if needed.

❄ Storage & reheating

Store the pesto in an airtight container in the refrigerator. It should last for up to 5 days. You can also freeze in an airtight container or freeze portions in ice-cube trays, then transfer to a freezer bag once frozen. Defrost in the refrigerator overnight, then use as per the recipe.

Coriander chilli pesto

50g (1¾oz) large bunch of fresh coriander (cilantro), leaves picked and longer stalks removed

1–2 jalapeños (depending on how hot you like it), sliced

2 garlic cloves, peeled

zest and juice of ½ lime

3 tablespoons pine nuts

30g (⅓ cup) grated (shredded) Parmesan

¼ teaspoon sea salt, plus extra to taste if needed

¼ teaspoon ground black pepper

90ml (⅓ cup) olive oil

1 Add the coriander, jalapeños, garlic, lime zest and juice, pine nuts, Parmesan, salt and pepper to a food processor and pulse for about 10 seconds to break up the garlic and pine nuts.

2 Turn the food processor back on and pour in the oil in a steady stream, which should take about 10 seconds. Check for consistency – if you like your pesto a little chunky, it's ready to go. If you like it smoother, whizz for another 10–20 seconds until the texture is to your liking.

3 Taste the pesto and add more lightly crushed sea salt if needed.

HOW TO USE

- Toss with spaghetti or pasta shapes.

- Drizzle on a creamy risotto.

- Spread onto chicken breasts, sprinkle on breadcrumbs and drizzle with oil before baking in the oven at 200°C fan/425°F/gas mark 7 for 25–30 minutes, until piping hot throughout and no longer pink in the middle.

- Use as a base sauce for pizza in place of tomato.

- Stir into tomato, bean or lentil soups for extra flavour.

- Smother on a chicken, steak or cheese sandwich.

- Use as part of my Baked gnocchi with chicken & red pesto (see page 67).

- Use as part of my Red pepper pesto pasta with feta (see page 23).

- Use as part of my Griddled lamb cutlets with coriander pesto (minus the chillies, see page 103).

Super Sauces

Creamy buffalo sauce

There's no getting around it, this is a spicy hot sauce! You can tone down the heat a little by reducing the hot sauce and increasing the cream, so that people who 'don't mind a bit of heat' will enjoy it too. But it will always have a kick to it – and I LOVE that! It's got a real depth of flavour, with a salty-spicy-creaminess, which makes me crave it so often. There's nothing like stirring it into a big bowl of penne and sitting on the sofa to devour the lot.

 Serves 4   **Prep time** 10 mins   **Cook time** 20 mins   **Total time** 30 mins

1 tablespoon oil
1 onion, peeled and diced
1 red (bell) pepper, deseeded and diced
1 yellow (bell) pepper, deseeded and diced
1 tablespoon Cajun spice mix
½ teaspoon ground black pepper
2 garlic cloves, peeled and minced
2 jalapeños (or medium heat green chillies), sliced
360ml (1½ cups) chicken stock
3 tablespoons hot pepper sauce
1 tablespoon Worcestershire sauce
1 tablespoon cider vinegar
120ml (½ cup) double (heavy) cream
50g (½ cup) grated Parmesan
1 tablespoon cornflour (cornstarch,) mixed with 3 tablespoons cold water to form a slurry (optional)

1. Heat the oil in a large frying pan (skillet) over a medium heat. Add the onion, red and yellow pepper, Cajun spice mix and black pepper. Fry for 5 minutes, stirring often, until the onion and peppers and slightly softened.

2. Stir in the garlic and jalapeños, then pour in the stock, hot pepper sauce, Worcestershire sauce and cider vinegar. Stir and bring to the boil, then simmer for 10 minutes until reduced by one-quarter.

3. Stir in the cream and Parmesan and heat through for a further minute.

4. If you want to thicken the sauce, slowly pour in the cornflour slurry, while stirring.

HOW TO USE

- Stir in cooked pasta and cooked chicken for buffalo chicken pasta.

- Add in vegetables, such as peas, chopped fine green beans, chopped courgette (zucchini), sugar snap peas (snow peas), tomatoes or mushrooms and cook in the sauce for 10 minutes. Serve over rice.

- Stir into cooked ramen or egg noodles and serve with halved soft-boiled eggs for a spicy noodle dish.

- Use to smother chicken wings or drizzle on chicken or pork kebabs.

- Spoon over cooked salmon and serve with rice, potatoes or pasta.

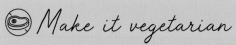 *Make it vegetarian*

Use vegetable stock instead of chicken stock, vegetarian Worcestershire sauce and replace the Parmesan with vegetarian Italian-style hard cheese.

Basic stir-fry sauce

If you know your way around a good stir-fry sauce you've got quick dinners in the bag! Add to crunchy stir-fried veg, meat or noodles – or all three – for a filling, nutritious dinner in no time. If you want to make it even faster, use prepared packs of sliced vegetables, cooked chicken and cooked noodles. It makes a shortcut dinner quicker to make than a microwave meal.

 Serves 4   Prep time 5 mins   Cook time 0 mins   Total time 5 mins

2 garlic cloves, peeled and minced
4 tablespoons light soy sauce
1 tablespoon cornflour (cornstarch)
2 tablespoons Chinese rice wine or mirin
3 tablespoons light brown sugar
3 tablespoons sweet chilli sauce
2 tablespoons tomato ketchup
120ml (½ cup) vegetable stock
1 tablespoon sesame oil

1   Put the garlic, soy sauce and cornflour into a jug and stir together until the cornflour is fully incorporated (the cornflour will help the sauce thicken when you come to heat it up).

2   Add the rice wine, sugar, sweet chilli sauce, ketchup, stock and sesame oil. Stir together to combine.

3   Use right away, or pour into a sealed container and refrigerate until needed (up to 2 weeks).

HOW TO USE
Stir-fry your vegetables/meat/noodles in a little oil and seasoning until cooked, then pour in this sauce and stir fry for 2–3 minutes until the sauce is hot and has thickened.

Nicky's pro tips
You can change the flavour profile of this sauce with a few tweaks. Add in 1 teaspoon of chilli (red pepper) flakes for more heat. Add in 1 tablespoon of tomato purée (paste) for a more 'tomatoey' flavour. Add fresh ginger and a squeeze of lemon juice for a zingier flavour.

Coconut curry sauce

££

A creamy, coconutty base curry sauce, made to the heat level of your choice.
I like to keep this in the freezer in single portions so it's quick to defrost and use.

 Serves 4   **Prep time** 10 mins   **Cook time** 20 mins   **Total time** 30 mins

1 onion, peeled and roughly chopped

2 garlic cloves, peeled

2 teaspoons minced ginger

3 tablespoons ghee or oil

3 tablespoons curry powder (mild, medium or hot, according to your preference)

½ teaspoon ground cinnamon

1½ teaspoons paprika

1 teaspoon tamarind paste

¾ teaspoon salt

½ teaspoon ground black pepper

400ml (1 ⅔ cups) passata

2 tablespoons tomato purée (paste)

1 x 400ml (14fl oz) can full-fat coconut milk

3 tablespoons desiccated (shredded) coconut

1. Add the onion, garlic and ginger to a food processor and blend to a paste.

2. Heat the ghee or oil in a large frying pan (skillet) over a high heat. Add the onion mixture and fry for 3–4 minutes, stirring occasionally, until starting to brown at the edges.

3. Reduce the heat to medium, then add the curry powder, cinnamon, paprika, tamarind, salt and pepper. Stir together and cook for 1 minute.

4. Add the passata, tomato purée, coconut milk and desiccated coconut. Stir and bring to the boil, then reduce the heat and simmer for 10–15 minutes, stirring occasionally, until slightly thickened.

HOW TO USE

Vegetarian

- Fry chunks of vegetables (such as courgette/zucchini, cooked potato, broccoli, broad (fava) beans), tofu or other vegetarian protein in a little oil until cooked. Season with salt and pepper then stir in the sauce and heat through.

- Add leftover cooked vegetables to the sauce and heat through.

- Stir into cooked noodles and serve with chopped boiled eggs for a quick egg noodle curry.

Non-vegetarian

- Fry chicken, steak or prawns (shrimp) or meatballs in a oil until cooked. Season with salt and pepper then stir in the sauce and heat through.

- Add leftover chopped cooked meat to the sauce and heat through.

- Spoon over cooked salmon and serve with rice for a speedy fish curry.

Nicky's pro tips

If you want to add chicken (for non-vegetarians), or vegetables (ideally ones with a 10–15-minute cook time, such as mushrooms, courgettes/zucchini small carrot chunks or green beans), add them in Step 3, then fry for 5 minutes, before adding the liquids.

Super Sauces

Quick bolognese sauce

Spag bol is an absolute staple in our house. I love to make a great big batch and freeze it in portions. Our go-to is to serve it with fresh tagliatelle, which only takes 5 minutes to cook. But if we fancy a change, it's easy to turn it into a spicy or creamy bolognese, or even repurpose it for chilli con carne or lasagne.

 Serves 4
 Prep time 5 mins
 Cook time 25 mins
 Total time 30 mins

1 tablespoon olive oil
1 onion, peeled and finely diced
1 celery stick, finely diced
3 garlic cloves, peeled and minced
500g (1lb 2oz) minced (ground) beef (10–20% fat for the best flavour)
3 tablespoons tomato purée (paste)
1 teaspoon dried oregano
½ teaspoon dried thyme
1 tablespoon Worcestershire sauce
1 beef stock (bouillon) cube, crumbled
2 x 400g (14 oz) cans finely chopped tomatoes
½ tablespoon light brown sugar
½ teaspoon salt
½ teaspoon ground black pepper

1 Heat the oil in a large frying pan (skillet) over a medium–high heat. Add the onion, celery and garlic and cook for 4–5 minutes until slightly softened.

2 Add the beef and cook for a further 4–5 minutes, breaking up any large clumps with a spatula, until browned.

3 Stir in the tomato purée, oregano, thyme, Worcestershire sauce and stock cube, then add the canned tomatoes, sugar, salt and pepper. Stir everything together and bring to the boil, then simmer for 10–15 minutes, stirring occasionally, until the sauce thickens slightly.

HOW TO USE

- Mix with spaghetti, tagliatelle, or other pasta shapes for a simple bolognese.

- Turn it into a spicy bolognese by adding 1–2 tablespoons of sriracha.

- Turn it into a creamy bolognese by adding 4 tablespoons of double (heavy) cream.

- Stir through cooked ravioli (it works well with cheese-filled ravioli) or gnocchi and serve immediately, or transfer to a baking dish and sprinkle with grated (shredded) cheese, then bake at 200°C fan/425°F/gas mark 7 for 15–20 minutes until the cheese is bubbling.

- Fry 2 teaspoons of ground cumin, 1 teaspoon of ground coriander and 1 teaspoon of hot chilli powder in 1 tablespoon of oil for 1 minute. Stir in a 400g (14oz) can of drained kidney beans, then add the bolognese sauce for a quick chilli con carne.

- Use as a jacket (baked) potato filling, topped with Cheddar and spring onions (scallions).

- Make into a quick lasagne by layering up the bolognese with fresh lasagne sheets and spoonfuls of ricotta. Top with grated cheese and bake in the oven at 180°C fan/400°F/gas mark 6 for 30–40 minutes, until the cheese is bubbling.

Nicky's pro tips

Batch cook this recipe, making double or triple the amount, so you can portion up and freeze for later. It will take a few minutes longer to fry the onions and beef and an extra 10–15 minutes of simmering – but it saves time on your next meal!

Make it vegetarian

Use vegetarian mince to replace the beef, replace the beef stock cube with a vegetable one and replace the Worcestershire sauce with a vegetarian version.

Index

Acknowledgements

First of all, I want to say a big thank you to my brilliant family. Chris, Gracey and Lewis – you're my biggest supporters and best taste-testers – even when you're faced with taste-tasting five different dishes that absolutely don't go together!

Chris, thank you for being the best husband and business partner a girl could ask for. I started listing out all the things I'm grateful for, but it got ridiculously long. You're my hero. Thank you x.

Kath (my mother-in-law), thank you for everything you do for us, from helping with our social media, looking after the kids and even doing our ironing to free up time for us. We love you so much (and thanks to Steve for letting us borrow her, entertaining the kids and inspiring us with your amazing allotment produce!).

Thank you to the whole team at Kyle - Judith Hannam (publishing director), Samhita Foria (project editor), Mathew Grindon (marketing), Ailie Springall (publicity), Paul Palmer-Edwards (designer), Emily Noto (production) and everyone else that helped in the production of this book. You're such a fab team and an absolute delight to work with.

To my literary agent, Emily Sweet, your help has been invaluable! From helping me with the vision, proposal, planning and publicity. Thank you, I couldn't have done it without you.

I also want to say a big thank you to my blog readers and social media followers on Kitchen Sanctuary. I appreciate you every day, for making my recipes, watching my videos, your kind comments and valuable input. I never would have been able to turn my hobby into a job that I'm grateful for every day without your continuous support.